Positive Thinking and Self-Esteem

How You Can Transform Negative Thinking into Self Love with the Right Mindset Habits, Self-Talk and Daily Affirmations

Contents

Part 1: Positive Thinking

The Ultimate Guide to Transforming Negative Thinking into Self Love with the Right Mindset Habits, Highly Effective Self Talk, Daily Affirmations and Success Thoughts

Introduction

Have you ever looked at yourself in the mirror and thought, "You look dreadful"? Have you ever turned down a challenge that would have been fun to do and brought you real satisfaction, because you thought, "I'll only go and screw it up, I'd be better off not trying in the first place?" Have you ever felt you're a bit of a failure--at work, at personal relations, at being popular, or smart, or coping?

Most of us have thoughts like that occasionally, and many of us think that's normal. But thoughts like these can, over time, sap your energy, close off opportunities, and even lead to depression. Negative thinking traps you in a vicious circle--because you expect failure, you don't take on challenges, or you set yourself up to fail. And when you fail, you believe that negative voice that told you failure was inevitable. But it's not true --and you *can* break out of that negative spiral, given the right insights and the right techniques.

Some people say negative thinking is realistic. "We're not all Shakespeare or Einstein," they say. They believe that positive thinking is airy-fairy, new age-y, methodologically unsound wishful thinking. But in fact, negative thinking isn't realistic. The little negative voice never gives a realistic assessment of your abilities, for instance, "okay, you're good at math, a bit less so at visualizing spatial concepts, and better at getting new accounts than chasing late payments". It's continually negative, and that's not helpful; it simply slows you down, stops you making a contribution to your job, family, or society in general, and makes you feel bad about yourself. Negative thinking is useless--more than that, it's damaging.

Some people think positive thinking is wishy-washy and dishonest. But positive thinking isn't about believing you can do *anything*. It's about concentrating on what you can do, rather than obsessing about what you can't. It's about being open to trying new activities, taking new opportunities, and learning new skills. It's about treating your failures as learning opportunities rather than disasters. It's about building the confidence that lets you feel it's okay not to succeed at every single thing you do, as long as you can learn and move on.

In this book, we're going to try to silence your inner critic--that little voice of doubt and negativity. We're going to show you some techniques for helping yourself feel more positive, and that has a whole load of benefits.

- You can easily come out of your comfort zone and try new activities or reach for a higher level of performance once you stop thinking "I can't do that".

- You can use visualization and affirmation techniques as tools to help you achieve your goals--without that inner critic predicting doom and disaster!

- You can feel better about yourself. That will help you be more relaxed, makes your life less stressful, and will help you get on with people much more easily.

- If you're the kind of person who feels you always need to prove yourself, you can stop feeling pressured. Positive thinking will take the pressure off.

- Feeling more relaxed will show in your body language. If you are more relaxed, you'll look more confident and at ease, and that will affect people's reactions to you for the better.

- Positive thinking helps you deal with life's disappointments. Rather than feeling down in the dumps and wondering why life treats you so badly, positive thinking will help you address problems and make plans to progress. Positive thinking won't change what life throws at you--but it will make you much, much better at coping and moving on.

- Positive thinking gives you freedom. It lets you try new things and make positive changes in your life.

- Feeling more compassionate towards yourself can also make you more compassionate towards others. You can actually become a better person by thinking more positively about yourself and about others.

- There's evidence that people who have a spiritual or meditative practice are, on average, healthier than those who don't and may even live longer.

By purchasing this book, you've already taken the first step towards breaking out of negative thinking and starting out on a positive future. Carry on reading, and we'll show you how to improve your life, start caring for yourself properly, and become a happier and perhaps better person.

Chapter 1 – What is Happiness? A Few Thoughts to get Started

What would it take to make you happy?

Professor Laurie Santos at Yale University teaches a class on happiness, and she takes her students through the question of what they need to be happy. Good grades? The right partner in life? A really lovely apartment or house? A great salary? Then she shows them the psychological studies which show that none of these things actually delivers happiness in the long term.

It's a fascinating exercise. But it shows that if you think that being happy is just about changing your circumstances, you'll never achieve happiness. There's an interesting mechanism in play, called *hedonic adaptation*, which means that once we get a certain level of material success, we adjust our desires upwards. The more you have, in other words, the more you want.

So, if happiness isn't about changing your circumstances--getting a higher salary, more 'stuff', a better lifestyle--what is it really about? It's really about *changing yourself* from the inside.

Positive thinking is about being happy with yourself. It's about freeing yourself from other people's expectations and judgments, and knowing who you are and what's important to you. It's about having confidence. All of that will deliver you a happier and better life.

All the scientific research that's been carried out on positive thinking, by the way, shows that positive thinkers tend to achieve success because of their attitude, rather than people's success leading to them being positive thinkers. You can probably think of more than one friend who has what most people would consider a successful career and marriage but is still the most miserable person you know!

Reasons to be Cheerful

There are good reasons why you should be cheerful. You might think, for instance, that if you get cancer, that's a bummer whether you are a pessimist or an optimist.

But in fact, a study carried out by Harvard's TH Chan School of Health published in *American Journal of Epidemiology* shows that your survival rate is probably higher if you're an optimist. This study followed 70,000 women over an eight- year period and analyzed their outcomes. Women who tended to have an optimistic view of their lives had a significantly reduced risk of dying from cancer, heart disease, stroke, respiratory disease, or infection over that period. Psychological resilience, it appears, can improve medical outcomes. That's a good reason to be cheerful.

There are even suggestions that positive thinking can boost the immune system. Segerstrom & Sephton, in *Psychological Science*, divided law students into two groups--those with "positive expectancies" and those who were more pessimistic. The optimists turned out far more able to resist the common cold than their pessimistic peers. Imagine--a bit of positive thinking actually *can* beat off an attack of flu!

These are not the only studies. A wide range of different research papers from 1953 to the present day show that positive thinkers are more likely to stay healthy for longer. On average, they live 7.5 years longer than miserable people!

Still not convinced? Look at what happens to people in their old age. The *Canadian Medical Association Journal* printed a study that showed that older people who enjoy their lives are up to 80% less likely to have problems with mobility, incontinence, or falling. If you think old age will be painful and humiliating, it's far more likely to happen to you than to someone with a more positive outlook. And if you have that positive outlook and want to enjoy a long and happy life, then you'll be cheered by another study in *JAMA* (Giltay, Kamphuis and Kalmijn) which shows that positive thinkers have a 55% less chance of dying early.

All in all, positive thinking has more health benefits than you'd think. Anyone who dismisses it as unrealistic, wishy-washy, New Age nonsense needs to take a look at the scientific journals!

Positive thinking can also make you less stressed. That message comes from a study at King's College, London (Eagleson, Hayes, Matthews, Perman, Hirsch, 2016). The study took a number of people with Generalized Anxiety Disorder and divided them into groups who practiced either rehearsing positive outcomes (as images or as verbal thoughts), or simply thinking about positive images that didn't relate to their anxiety. A month later, *all* groups reported significant reductions in their anxiety levels. So, as long as you are practicing positive thinking of some kind, it's of benefit--even if it doesn't seem to be directly relevant to your problems.

That means simply repeating an affirmation, like "I am strong, I am smart," can help you, even though your problem right now is being in a job you don't like, not having enough money, or having been diagnosed with rheumatoid arthritis. Even thinking about images that you find positive, like a beautiful sunset or an athlete breasting the tape, will have a benefit on your stress levels and make your life much more enjoyable.

And by the way, positive thinking isn't just for snowflakes, bleeding heart liberals, and soccer moms. The military reckons it works--the US Army now teaches positive thinking using the Penn Resilience Program to increase the 'mental fitness' of its officers. They learn coping mechanisms as well as positive thinking, and the program is now taught as a preventative against PTSD.

Why negative thinking hurts you

If you are living with negative thinking, you're living in a world which you see as a negative space. You'll look for negative outcomes, and that may lead to you behaving in ways that help to create those negative outcomes.

For instance, if you see every comment as a criticism, and every criticism as an attempt to hurt you or humiliate you, you're closing off a huge range of learning opportunities. You'll come across as defensive and bristly when people try to give you feedback, so eventually, some of your friends and colleagues may not bother.

Suppose you've just repainted your front door, and your neighbor says "Oops, there's a little run in the paint right at the top; it must have dripped when you were painting it."

- Do you say--"Well, I bet you couldn't do it any better!"

- Or is your response--"Do you know how I could fix it?"

That's just a small example of how a positive thinker could end up getting more out of life. You never know, your neighbor might even offer to fix the problem and teach you how to stop drips happening in the first place.

Negative thinking can also prevent you taking advantage of the many opportunities life offers you. For instance, some people let low self-esteem prevent them from applying for promotion. Some people can't break out of their comfort zone, even when they know they'd enjoy doing something if they could get past their anxieties. Often, when we're thinking negatively, we decide not to do something because there's a chance we might fail. But if you decide not to do something, of course, you *have* failed!

- "I'm not going to go on a diet, because I know I won't have the self-discipline to stick to it."

- "There's no point to my saving money. I'll never manage to save enough to buy my own house."

- "I'm not going to audition for that role; they'll never give it to me."

Positive thinkers would ask what's the downside. None! And the potential upside? Even if you don't stick to your diet, just having a slightly healthier eating regime could help you shed a few pounds and feel better. Even if you don't save a house deposit, you might have enough to fund a vacation, a business of your own, or an RV. And even if you don't get the role, there could be all kinds of benefits. Someone might think you'd be ideal for a different role, you might get an offer of coaching, and you'll have more confidence.

If you break out of the negative thinking rut - if you believe you deserve to be happy - you'll take the opportunities that can help you achieve happiness. You'll also, more than likely, make the people around you also feel happy, and that creates a virtuous circle...

Chapter 2 – Breaking the Vicious Circle

Negative thinking and negative emotions, unfortunately, are really good at clinging on to us, like poison ivy. It's easy to get locked into negative emotions. It's easy for negative thinking to turn a small setback into a major catastrophe.

For instance, you manage to knock your coffee over at breakfast. It's really easy to let that put you in a negative frame of mind; it's only 8 am and already the day is a bad one. What will go wrong next? You'll probably miss your bus and be late for work, the boss will probably want to see you about that report you were late submitting... Before you know it, you're in a vicious circle of negative thinking.

But you *can* break out. For instance, instead of fuming, you could instead say, "Well, I've already wiped up an impressive amount of coffee and changed my shirt and pants. What other superpowers might I have to call on today?" Or you could think of the chances you have to make the rest of the day turn out better-- having lunch with an old friend, getting an article finished, playing bowls this evening, or listening to some great music on the way to work.

Negative thinking is even worse when it involves other people. Suppose your partner managed to upset the coffee. You start shouting and try to make them feel guilty, and that's going to make things worse.

On the other hand, if you manage to react calmly and ask for help wiping up and perhaps making another cup of coffee, you'll probably get an apology, a fresh coffee, and even a hug.

But it does take practice to manage to approach everything in a positive-thinking way. If you're used to negative thinking, it will take a while, and you'll need to work at it. You'll need practice because it's not something you can change at a superficial level. Negative thinking has been wired into your brain at a subconscious level, so you have to change the way your brain flips its switches.

The good news is that once you've done that, positive thinking becomes automatic. That will bring huge benefits to your life. So, in this book, we're going to help you *train your subconscious* to work for you instead of against you.

Let's start with the micro level--breaking out of a negative emotional state, such as feeling angry or frightened.

Breathe!

Yes, it really is true--just taking a deep breath can help diffuse negative emotions. But you need to do it properly. If you take a deep breath and then hold it, you'll be tensing your body up, and that will make things worse. Take a big deep breath and then breathe out slowly, emptying your lungs and feeling that you're expelling some of that negative feeling with your breath.

Better?

One of the reasons that negative emotions can get such a hold of us is that they dominate our physical sensations too. Think of times that you've had one of the following sensations;

- "butterflies in your tummy"
- feeling shaky or trembling
- your heart beating very fast
- being short of breath
- feeling tearful
- hyperventilating
- feeling hot and flushed and even breaking out in a sweat
- realizing that you were gripping something so hard it felt painful.

Sensations like these are very powerful. They are so powerful that they can turn you inwards and stop you perceiving what's actually happening around you. And they are so powerful that they will perpetuate your negative thinking too.

Although we divide up the different negative emotions into fear, anger, sadness, and so on, many of their physical manifestations are similar. Breaking out of the negative emotion is much easier once you recognize those physical feelings and dispel them.

A deep breath helps. When you breathe in, you're making sure your body isn't starved of oxygen. But when you breathe out, you're helping to relax your entire body. Try it now--while you're feeling 'normal', not scared or stressed--and feel how when you breathe out slowly, your shoulders drop down a little, your back feels more relaxed, and your whole body seems to let go a little.

Positive thinking is really helped by some physical training. Train your body to relax. Meditation or yoga can be a help, but you can start this very minute by just taking time to do one of these short exercises:

• breathe in and out slowly, and notice your breath. What does it feel like? How deep in your body does the air go? When you breathe out, what do you feel in your stomach, your throat, your back, your arms? Just concentrate on breathing. Start with just ten to twelve good long breaths and finish once you feel refreshed.

• Just sit down and feel whether your fingers are tense or relaxed. Can you relax them more? What about your arms? Your shoulders? Your neck? Your toes? Your feet? Try to feel the most relaxed that you can.

• Do some 'warm-ups' just like actors do before they go on stage. Gently move your head--look down, then up; move your head to the left, then the right; roll it around on your shoulders. Try to feel really loose and floppy. Move your arms to make them really loose. Wiggle your fingers. Stand up and flop right over--it doesn't matter whether you can touch your toes, what matters is that your back feels stretched and your whole body feels relaxed. Stand up again and feel the difference. You should be energized and happy.

• Try making yourself very tense and then very relaxed. Make your hand into a tight fist, then spring your fingers loose and relax. Hunch your shoulders up like Muttley the Dog in Wacky Races laughing, then relax them. Make your arms really rigid, then let them flop loose. Feel the difference.

Every time you carry out one of these exercises, you build feelings of relaxation and well-being that your body will remember. It's just like a musician building 'muscle memory' by practicing scales. When you need to break out of a negative emotion, your body will help you, because it can remember how to relax. And you know how to get yourself into relaxation mode. That's a really powerful way to break out of negative thoughts and feelings.

Challenging negative thoughts

Now let's look at the macro level of challenging negative thinking. A negative thought is only powerful when you don't recognize it or challenge it.

So, take stock of your thoughts. Learn to recognize negative thoughts, whether they manifest as self-criticism ("Why am I always so clumsy?"), pessimism ("These things never work out") or cynicism ("Of course, they're all on the take"). Recognize the way negative thinking tries to get you to interpret things in a skewed, negative way, or to take things personally.

For instance, you hear people laughing and immediately you think they're laughing *at you.* Challenge that thought! Why would they be laughing at you? What are they actually laughing at? Is that a nasty laugh or a happy laugh? Sometimes, friends might laugh when they see you because they were just thinking about you and look, you've turned up--what a coincidence!

Let's take a second step from just challenging those negative thoughts, and try to replace them with something more positive.

So, what else might you have thought when you heard laughter? You might have thought "Someone sounds happy," or "I wonder if I can join in?" You might have thought that someone is having fun. You might have thought that people are enjoying each other's company. All of those thoughts are positive ways to react.

Tomorrow, just try systematically catching those negative thoughts and replacing them straight away by positive alternatives. Replace your fear and anger by optimism, excitement, and confidence.

Even negative situations can be approached in a positive way. Suppose you're involved in a car accident that's not your fault. That's negative. But you can approach it in a positive way. It's not your fault, and it's not addressed by the world personally to mess you up; no-one did it on purpose, it's just something that happened.

Take a deep breath, then respond calmly. Are you okay? Yes. Well that's good, isn't it? Is everyone else okay? What can you do to help? What needs to happen next? Whether it's calling the police, filling in insurance details, or sitting a shocked person down and holding their hand for a while till they feel able to manage, you'll be able to manage it.

Recognize distortions in the way you think about the world

Now we're going to look at a much more macro way of breaking the vicious circle of negative thinking--changing core beliefs that are holding you back. We all have core beliefs that we may not even realize are there lurking in the background, but which affect the way we see the world. You might believe "people from a working-class background can never get on in life", or "I'll never make a success of my career"; you might feel clumsy and uncoordinated, or have an unreasonable fear of dogs.

Negative thinking distorts reality. You need to recognize those distortions by checking the facts and then rebalancing your thoughts.

(You could say positive thinking distorts reality too. But it does so *in your favor*, like 'tilt' on a pinball machine.)

So, for example, you're from a poor background, and you think working class people never get on in the world. Do some research--find people from poor backgrounds who have succeeded in business, politics, the arts, technology. You might find that they shared particular challenges, but now that you've attacked the negative thought, you can look at how they overcame them and make plans for doing the same yourself.

Or if you think you'll never be a success--why do you believe that? You could think about all the skills that you have. Or you could think about what's holding you back, but positively, working out how to address these issues--with training, a change of approach, or getting a mentor who can help you, for instance.

Instead of having negative thoughts, try to build positive expectations. If you're going in for a race, and you know you're outclassed, you have a choice. You can think, "I can't win". That's not going to make running the race much fun. Or you can think, "I can be good, I can beat my personal best". One beginner decided, when she ran her first 5k, to focus on just one thing--"I will keep going, I can finish the course." And she did.

Positive expectations will encourage you to take the right risks. A writer submitted a story to a very prestigious competition. He didn't win. But he got a personal letter from one of the judges, asking him to contribute to an anthology and giving him real encouragement. If he'd listened to that negative little voice that said his story wasn't quite good enough, he would never have received that boost.

Impostor syndrome

Have you ever had the feeling that you don't really understand what you're doing--that you got your job by sheer luck, that you're a fake or a flake?

You're not the only one. Impostor syndrome is a well-known psychological problem. Even very successful people often feel that they don't really deserve their success.

There's a mechanism that enables them to believe it. If they work really hard, they put their success down simply to hard work. They can then continue to believe that they are not talented or smart, just hard working. And if they don't work particularly hard, but they are successful even so, they put it down to luck. They just got lucky-- they were in the right place at the right time, made a single good call, knew the right person to ask.

Look at how that mechanism works. Isn't it amazing how good we are at creating logical structures solely intended to keep us feeling bad about ourselves?

So, watch out for bad logic. For instance, generalizations. You have had two bad experiences when you panicked in an exam and wrote down the wrong answer. "I'm bad at exams!" you say, and you make that part of your identity. And you know what? You actually *make* yourself bad at exams by making yourself fearful and stressed. But you'd never base a statistic or a scientific study on just two cases of something happening. A more positive thought would be to say, "I was coping all right until I panicked. So how can I stop myself panicking in future?"

Perhaps, when you think about it, you had a late night before both those exams and weren't feeling your best. Perhaps they were on subjects you hadn't prepared. Or perhaps you had some other stress going on in your life at the time. Rather than generalize, think about the specific situations and try to find a positive route to improvement.

Watch out for exaggerations. Lots of people say "I'm bad at math" when what they mean is "I'm really good at languages and social sciences, but my math is not quite as good." Sometimes that means they're still in the top decile for math--which is not bad! The trouble is, you'll start believing that exaggeration and make it part of your identity, and that will limit your options.

Watch out for catastrophizing. That's when you pile negative on negative. Remember the spilled coffee at breakfast? Your mind races away. You spilled the coffee, you had to get changed, you'll miss your bus, you'll be late at work, the boss will see you're late, you'll get fired, you'll lose your house... Just deal with one thing at a time! Negative thinking always wants to pile up the misery--just refuse it, politely. One thing *doesn't* always lead to another.

Recognizing the truth

Sometimes the negative voice is a sign of something you need to hear. But it's not telling you the truth. You need to note that it's piped up, however you need to think hard about what's really behind it.

Let's give an example. One violinist played a rehearsal very badly and was getting stressed about his performance in the concert scheduled for three days later. He'd always enjoyed performing, and he'd always performed well up till then. He realized he was actually beginning to tell himself that he had always been lucky till this point, that he'd always played easy music, that he wasn't actually all that great.

Instead of listening to those negative thoughts, he tried to work out why he was feeling stressed. There was nothing new about the situation of performing, and it was with other musicians he knew and had played with before. He knew the piece. He should have felt happy with it. But ... actually, he felt a little under-prepared.

And as soon as he said that to himself, he knew what the problem *really* was. He went and practiced--two hours that day, four hours for the next two days. He played through his pieces fast, slowly, phrase by phrase and all the way through, from the music and from memory. When he walked onto the stage on concert day, he told himself that he was the best prepared he'd ever been. He played a great concert, but better than that, he experienced no stress at all. He just enjoyed playing--the way he always had before.

He realized that he was only stressed because he wasn't well enough prepared, and he did exactly what he needed to do.

Let's move on

We've now given you techniques for addressing those negative thoughts as they crop up. We've shown you how far from being 'realistic' negative thoughts are and how often they distort reality. After all, what's more realistic, saying "all of a sudden I'm a really bad violinist," or "I need to do some more practice"? When negative thoughts come into your mind, you can now challenge them and start to replace them with more positive approaches.

But negative beliefs are often wired into us from a very early age. These kinds of beliefs are much more difficult to shift than a single negative thought. In the next chapter, we're going to look at how to deal with negative thinking in the longer term. Look at your mind as an overgrown garden--full of potential to grow beautiful flowers and fruit, but first, you have to learn how to pull up and eradicate your mental weeds.

Chapter 3 – Where Does Negativity Come From?

Negative beliefs all come from somewhere. You may have acquired them during your childhood, from things your parents told you, from bad experiences like being bitten by a dog or bullied at school.

Maybe your parents said things like "What makes you so special?" or "You're only doing it to get attention." One woman who had low self-esteem and felt she didn't deserve her success eventually tracked part of the problem down to a saying of her mother's--"Those who ask, don't get."

Most people say, "Those who *don't* ask, don't get." But whether her mother just mangled the proverb, or really believed that children who asked for something shouldn't be given it, that woman got the idea that if she wanted something, she shouldn't mention it. That if she wanted something, she didn't deserve it. It took a long time for her to tackle that negativity but finding out how it had first gotten lodged in her brain was a major breakthrough.

Sometimes it's a bad experience that leaves its imprint deep in your brain. Were you lonely at a boarding school or camp? Were you really afraid of something, but not allowed to show it or made fun of when you did? Were you scolded for not being 'normal'? Or for not being 'lady-like'? Did your mother once put you out of the car when you were naughty and tell you "You can walk home"? Or can you remember a time when you were in real pain, perhaps after falling over or getting hurt by a bigger child, but no one believed you?

Although such experiences may have left their mark, you might have to do quite a bit of thinking to track them down. Negative thinking has a way of concealing its entry points and hiding its trail. That's one of the things that makes it so resilient and so dangerous. You might even find that your parents have forgotten the event that you remember so clearly. It wasn't important *to them*. But it *is* to you!

This may sound like psychotherapy. It isn't. It's more like forensics--being a detective, finding out where your beliefs and feelings come from.

"Money is the root of all evil" - a case in point

One otherwise successful businesswoman had a very negative attitude toward money. She was well off, but she didn't invest her money. She was pretty frugal most of the time but sometimes would go off on a spending binge. She never knew quite how much money was in her bank account, and she never opened her statements. Eventually, a comment from one of her finance staff made her decide to work out why.

She'd grown up in a family where money was always short. Quite a few times, bad news was explained by statements like "your father needs to find a job" or "your mother has to help keep us afloat". The need for money explained why they had to move to a smaller house, why her parents couldn't come to her school concert or sports day, why she had to let herself in the house every evening and wait for her parents to come back from work, and why she couldn't have new books or go on school trips.

Her parents were always saying things like "money doesn't grow on trees" and "I'm not made of money." She made a vow that when she grew up, she'd never be short of money, and that propelled her career. But those negative beliefs and the fear of the money running out stayed lurking at the back of her mind.

Like her, you may have a very negative attitude to money. You may think you don't deserve to be well off. You may even feel that money was the root of your family's problems. Or you may fear losing it so much that you don't use your capital to invest in your business or your home, but you pile up savings that generate almost no interest in the bank.

Now, if you work out where those beliefs have come from, you've already come a step on the way to challenging them and moving on from your negative thinking to a more positive approach. The next step is to notice how those beliefs are limiting your choices.

- Do you actually have enough money to retire, or take a sabbatical, but you're still working because "I might need the money"? Your negative thinking has taken away your freedom!

- Do you find that every quarrel with family and friends is started by feeling that they're taking financial advantage of you? Your negative thinking is damaging those relationships.

- Do you spend nights worrying about whether the stock market will crash, whether you'll be able to pay off your home loan, whether you have enough in your IRA to retire? Your negative beliefs are stressing you out.

- Do you want to take a challenging job that you'd really enjoy, but the lower salary puts you off? That might be the right decision but not if it's purely motivated by your negative thinking about money.

- You don't put your wealth to productive use. You don't invest it. Your money could be making you richer. but instead, your negative beliefs are keeping you poor.

Once you notice how negative thinking limits your choices and actually impoverishes you, you've called its bluff. You know that it's not on your side, that it doesn't represent what's real. And you can now start to change.

Fight and flight

Negative thinking is often allied to fear, and fear works on parts of your brain, like the amygdala, that are constituted to deal with life in the prehistoric wild. That means fear bypasses your conscious, thinking, rational brain. (It's like bypassing the dialogues 'do you want to shut down now' and 'do you want to save this file' by yanking the computer cable out of the wall.)

Fear floods you with adrenaline and evokes two responses: "fight or flight". The idea is that either you club the attacking saber-tooth tiger to death, or you run for your life--you don't have time to stand still. We all have muscular and cerebral responses wired into us that come from way, way back in prehistory.

The difficulty is that 'fight or flight' responses are triggered not just by saber-tooth tigers or charging aurochs, but also by

- your teacher giving you a poor grade
- your boss asking you to step into her office
- opening a letter from your bank
- someone cutting you up at an intersection.

Because of the adrenaline and because your body is tensing ready for action, your brain is putting you into a state of stress. Negative thoughts and emotions can invoke this reaction, putting you into emergency mode. You'll end up being stressed all the time--far more than is warranted by the situations you actually find yourself in. That's bad for your health, it's bad for your relationships, and it's bad for your self-esteem.

Not only does emergency mode stress you to the max, it also narrows your mind. You might say it "focuses your thoughts"--and if you're faced by a saber-tooth tiger, you need to be pretty focused--but it closes down your access to the rational, think-it-through bit of your mind. And in a world that presents many more different opportunities and problems that require much more complex solutions than in the Neolithic age, that's really not helpful.

Negative emotions can push you into becoming a one-track thinker. You feel anger, fear, and stress, and you can't think clearly. You don't think about different interpretations of what's happening, or different options for tackling a problem. You can't think about the huge range of opportunities that lie in front of you.

Barbara Frederickson carried out a fascinating study in which she first showed different groups of people a range of film clips and then asked them to carry out a simple task. She showed some people movies that incited positive emotions; other people were shown neutral clips; and a third group watched movies that were designed to elicit negative emotions. Then she gave everyone a paper with the phrase 'I would like to...' at the top, and 20 blank lines underneath.

People who had been exposed to positive emotions wrote down by far the most responses--they had plenty of things they would like to do. Their brains were not possessed by negative emotions like anger or fear, and they could think about their choices and about the possibilities that were open to them. Their minds were open and clear. They were open to opportunity.

Subjects who had been exposed to negative emotions wrote down the fewest responses. They couldn't think of anything they would like to do. Their minds had closed them off from the world--in a prison of their own making.

That's why it's so important that you tackle negative emotions. Remember the exercises you did in the last chapter to learn how to relax, how to still your mind, and how to breathe? They're important because they tackle the physical manifestations of negative emotions--the adrenaline and tenseness--and help you regain the openness and calmness you need.

Dealing with fear

Fear can end up running your life. If you've always wanted to travel, but you're afraid of flying, fear is standing in the way of one of your dreams. But dealing with fear can be difficult. None the less, there are a number of ways you can start to do it.

A few people just go out and face it down. They buy a ticket, get on a plane, and suffer--and they're through. They are really brave. Most of us aren't like that. So, look for a way to deal with your fear in a controlled way, in a safe environment, and look for all the resources you can to help you do it.

For instance, with fear of flying, controlled ways to deal with that fear could be:

- looking at YouTube videos of airplane cockpits, of planes flying, of passengers arriving safely at an airport

- finding out whether you can sit in an aircraft simulator at a flying school

- going to an airport with a viewing platform and looking at the planes taking off and landing

- talking to a pilot about how planes work, how air traffic control works, how pre-flight checks are done

- These are all safe and controlled ways for you to take your brain for a walk, get it to look at the fear, and come away feeling that you can deal with it.

- Creating a safe environment might also mean, when you take your first flight,

- asking a friend to come along and being honest with them about your fear and your need for reassurance

- telling one of the flight assistants that you're very nervous and would appreciate their help in managing your fears

You should also work out where that fear comes from. Is it linked to a fear of heights, for instance? Are you afraid because when you're in a plane, you have no control over what's happening, or because you don't understand the different noises you hear and the different announcements being made? Or do your fears relate to having seen disaster movies? Addressing your fear in each of those cases would need different treatment.

One very scared passenger was worried by the perpetual 'ping' of the chimes on the plane. He always thought they were announcing some kind of emergency to cabin crew that passengers weren't allowed to know about. He also was worried by the fact that occasionally it sounded as if the engines had lost power or even been turned off. On one flight, he had a panic attack and ended up talking to the copilot about his fears.

He found out that while the chimes *might* mean that there was turbulence ahead, giving the cabin crew a chance to lock up their trolleys and perhaps head for a seat, chimes might also mean that the plane was at 10,000 feet altitude, that a passenger had a medical problem needing assistance, or ... that the pilot wanted a coffee!

As for the drop-in engine noise, that meant the plane was reducing speed, for instance when it reached 'TD', the top of its descent path. The pilot explained how speed and required engine power related to the different phases of the flight. Understanding these things helped the nervous flier to become more at ease. Now, if he feels himself getting nervous, he says "TD" under his breath, or "pilot wants a coffee", and smiles.

Bring reality to battle against fear!

Challenge your fear by considering the reality. That might mean comparing plane accidents to road traffic accidents. In fact, the odds of a plane crash are one for every 1.2 million flights. (Have you taken a million flights yet?) Your chances of dying in a plane crash are one in 11 million, while your chances of dying in a car crash are one in 5,000.

You're afraid of taking your driving test because you're worried you will fail. Look at the consequences. So, if you fail, what happens? You just have to take it again. That's not a catastrophe, so your fear is disproportionate. Now look at the stats (in this case for examinees in the UK). Only about 50% of people pass first time. That means that you have an evens chance of passing the test. Nearly 50% of second-time examinees pass. That means about three-quarters of people pass either first or second time.

Then ask if there's anything you can do to change the odds. For instance, some driving test centers have much higher pass rates-- usually rural areas where traffic isn't so fast moving or so dense as in town. Some reasons for failure make up a very high percentage of failures, and are easily avoided--for instance, exceeding the speed limit.

Making a safe space

In the theater, actors often have to handle emotions that they find difficult or painful to express. Sometimes they have to engage physically with other actors, such as in a fight scene. That can be painful unless it is well managed and unless all the actors know they can trust each other.

That's why directors and teachers in the theater work hard to create a "safe space" where actors can handle difficult emotions or experiment with physical theater without feeling at risk. For instance, some directors use trust exercises, where, for instance, one actor is supported by a 'cradle' of the other actors' arms, or where one actor is blindfolded and is guided around the room by the others.

You need to create your own safe space too. Find friends that you know you can rely on to help you combat your fears and negative emotions. Be honest with them if you're finding it difficult.

You might put limits on what you're going to do right now. For instance, if you're feeling panicky about social situations, for whatever reason, you might say, "I'm only going to go out one night this week, and I'll visit a bar where the owner is a friend and can make sure I'm okay." If you're worried about driving after you had an accident, you might say "I'm going to drive to the supermarket and back, but I won't take the car to work this week." Those limits are there just like training wheels, to stop you doing too much. They're there to help you get started without taking the risk of a set-back. When you can handle more, revise your limits.

Part of making a safe space is allowing yourself to fail, which we'll talk about more in a later chapter. An artist who wants to learn a new technique or a musician learning a new song needs to accept that the first few attempts will be failures. That's part of the learning curve. In this case, it's just about putting your normal expectations of success aside for a little while.

In other cases, you may need to think about safe ways to limit the consequences of failure. For instance, if you want to launch your own business, you might decide to use Kickstarter or to do a pilot project rather than jumping in with both feet.

"As if"

"As if" can be a very powerful pair of words.

- Let's play this music as if I'm not in front of an audience
- let's take this test as if the results don't matter
- let's just behave as if everything's fine.

You're not denying the fear. You're just deciding to *pretend* that it's not there--or re-framing the circumstances so that it *shouldn't* be there.

You might restate what you want to achieve. If you are facing a music exam and you feel that you need to play a piece faultlessly, why don't you think about really bringing out the emotion of the music instead? That takes the pressure off. If you have a mock exam to take, stop thinking about the pass rate and think instead about managing the exam process--doing your revision, getting a good night's sleep, arriving with the right gear, reading the questions properly, and planning your answers.

On the trail of negativity

Tracking the negative all the way back to its sources is like discovering the source of the Nile. You need to be a determined explorer of your own psyche!

There are several things that can tip you off to negative beliefs that have wired themselves into your brain. For instance, look for recurring patterns. Why are they happening? You might need to challenge the first answer that comes up--it's likely to be a piece of negative thinking.

You have a string of bad relationships, and your first answer to the question of why that happens is, "There's something wrong with me."

Do some more analysis. What else did those relationships have in common? What was the thing that made each one fail? Was it the same? It could be that you have just had bad luck, or it might be that, for instance, your partners couldn't cope with your long working hours.

You are known for having a bad temper. You say of yourself, "I have a low flash-point." Again and again, you flip, and lash out, when something goes wrong. So again, there's a recurring pattern.

Look at each event. What happened *before* you lost your temper? What triggers it? You may find that there's a specific trigger--"people not taking me seriously", for instance. Does that relate to a feeling of neediness or low self-esteem? Why is it important to you that people take you seriously?

Look at events that *didn't* trigger your temper even though things went badly wrong. Why not? What was different?

Now look at *what you did next*. Did that change how you felt about the event? Did that change how other people reacted? For instance, when you walked out of the room for five minutes, then came back and apologized for losing your temper, did people accept that apology happily? Did they then listen to you when you talked about how to move on? Did you get a better outcome?

Think about what these recurring patterns say about you. Again, avoid negative thinking. Your losses of temper don't just mean "I'm an angry person." Ask what you are angry *about*. What kind of things flip your 'rage' button? Is it unfairness and injustice? Is it being belittled? Is it when you screw up something you ought to be able to do? Is it waste? (Some people get really angry about waste or about throwing anything away. That might go back to being told as children, that they had to eat everything on their plate.)

Once you've worked out what you're angry about, you can ask whether you need to be so angry about it. For instance, you 're a successful business owner but you still hate sitting in front of your bank manager because you feel so powerless. It makes you feel like a child again. It makes you really angry when you're treated as if you are unimportant and a nuisance.

But actually, you don't need to be so angry. It's not personal; your bank manager may just be someone who treats the rest of the world like that. (You could always move banks.) Or next time you feel angry at being talked down to, you could say something like this, "I don't think you give me enough credit for running a successful business. I do understand how the financial markets work. I just need to know what the criteria are for deciding whether to make this loan so I can see if I meet them."

Absolutism

Negative thinking often digs its claws into us by sinking an absolute statement far beneath our conscious thoughts. Try tracking every negative thought back to the absolute statement that it refers to--"the world is unfair," "I am worthless," "life is hard".

Absolute thinking is very damaging. It can stop us reacting to things in an appropriate manner, and it can dictate what we do in a very harmful way. American psychologists Fiske and Taylor invented the concept of the *cognitive miser*, to describe the kind of person who takes short cuts in their thinking. Nuance and complexity take up processing time in our brains, and that's processing time the cognitive miser doesn't want to waste. Biases, prejudices and absolute negative thoughts are always there when we try to cut the neural cost of dealing with life.

But as so often happens when we try to save money, time, or effort, that saving comes with a cost. That cost doesn't just come in the form of a reduced ability to cope with complex or nuanced situations. It also comes with a cost to our mental health. A study by the University of Reading showed that absolutist words and absolute thinking correlate very markedly with depression. anxiety, and feelings of stress. The researchers have suggested that absolute thinking can in fact play a part in causing depressive episodes.

So, you need to challenge absolute thinking. One way to do this is simply to think of exceptions to the absolute rule. So, for instance if you think "I am worthless", then you can challenge that by thinking of examples of times when you contributed something to a group, when you did something remarkable or praiseworthy, or simply managed to help someone else. You can think of times that other people recognized your contribution by thanking you or by praising you. And when you add all these exceptions together, you can see you are *not* worthless. You are valued by other people, and maybe now you can start to value yourself.

Absolute thinking also encourages us to look at situations as black or white as really bad or really good with very little in between. In fact, life is mainly in between. Most things come in 50 Shades of Grey! The big problem with absolute thinking is that it makes a huge demand on life. It says "every day has to be really great," and you have to get everything right, or else *everything's* been ruined and it's totally worthless. So, for example when you get A grades on everything except for one paper, then absolute thinking says your academic performance is bad. It encourages you to focus on that one failure. I used the word "failure" there but in fact it might just be a B grade on one paper which isn't that bad. But absolute thinking has you saying "hey I bombed" instead of just "I guess I could improve that a little".

With many of us, that kind of black and white thinking can be tracked back to our parents. If you remember being told once when you misbehaved that you "ruined the whole day", or if you remember your parents being hypercritical of your school reports and always focusing on the negatives, that may be one reason that you're still stuck with absolute thinking.

One way that you can challenge black and white thinking is to keep a diary. Rather than just journaling a stream of consciousness, as it were, use two pages for every day. Use the page on the left to sum up what you think today. Then the next day use the page on the right to assess yesterday's thoughts now that you have let some time elapse. Over time you will probably find that your initial thoughts (that a day had been a complete disaster) are very often qualified or even reversed when you go back to look at what actually happened.

You may have found some explanation for things that happened which at first you thought were very negative. For instance: your boss wasn't interested in the report that you spent a week putting together. Yesterday, you wrote down that if your boss isn't interested in any contribution that you make to the business, you'll probably lose your job in the end. But suppose at work today you found out that the firm had just lost a big contract, and your boss was running around trying to save the other business that you had with that customer. Now you can understand that the underwhelmed reaction to your report doesn't mean your boss isn't interested in your contribution; it just means that yesterday was not the right day for getting his full attention.

Don't just write down that explanation on the right-hand page though. Also write a note to yourself. Remind yourself that you jumped to a negative conclusion which wasn't, in fact, the right one. Remind yourself that before you come to a conclusion, you ought to consider all the data. And then ask yourself why you jumped to that conclusion. Why did you let negative thinking get hold of your brain? What is the absolute belief to which that related? Now that you know the real facts about the individual situation, does that make you more or less likely to give credence to that absolute belief?

Writing things down is very powerful by the way. When we write things down, we are re-enacting them, and performing an action has a powerful impact on our minds. But also, for many of us, writing slows us down and creates a little distance between us and a situation. That distance can be very helpful when we're thinking about things that may link to our emotions or about beliefs that are deeply buried in our subconscious.

Other sources of negativity

Unfortunately, some people don't just allow their negative thinking to affect their own lives; they also inflict it on other people.

You probably know someone whose outlook is always negative. Their friends may even treat that as a bit of a joke--"Look at Jonathan! He always expects the sky to fall on his head!"

The trouble comes when that person starts talking about *your* plans and *your* life.

Imagine one university professor whose mother is a source of the following advice on the various career opportunities she's had presented to her over the past few years:

- I wouldn't take that job at Harvard--you might not get tenure.

- It doesn't matter how much you publish; there'll always be someone smarter than you.

- Don't go to India for that conference; it's full of Indians! You won't like it!

- Are you sure it's a good idea to take a sabbatical? They might not let you come back.

It's really time that either she stopped telling her mother anything about her career decisions, or told her mother that she's not going to listen to any advice. Because this isn't good career advice--it's all negative thinking.

That's an extreme case, but I bet when you read at least one of those sentences, you nodded your head and thought of someone who had given you exactly the same kind of advice. Friends who tell you to 'settle' rather than follow your dream, who tell you "you're not all that great", or who point out the negative aspects of anything you plan, for example.

It sounds horrible to say it, but people like that are not really your friends. You need to recognize them and their motivations. Sometimes they're driven by jealousy, sometimes by their own fears. They may not want you to succeed because they would feel threatened, or because they fear that if, say, you get in to a prestigious university and move away, you won't want to be friends with them anymore. Maybe their negative mindsets just mean they can't join in with your enthusiasm for a project. If they've invested their entire lives in believing that they can't or shouldn't pursue their dreams, seeing you do it can be emotionally threatening.

Clarinetist Eric Abramovitz's girlfriend actually went so far as to fake an email telling him he'd been rejected from the Colburn Conservatory, though he'd actually been awarded a place. She didn't want him to move away. A court awarded him more than $260,000 in damages once he discovered the fraud.

That's an extreme case. And you probably can cope with supporting a few friends who are pessimistic, as long as they don't become total nay-sayers. But learn to recognize this kind of negativity and where it comes from.

Once you've broken free of your own negative thinking, you might be able to see where your friends' negative thinking comes from. You might actually be more compassionate and be able to help them break free of it. But sometimes, you just have to avoid people that you know are going to pour cold water on all your plans. And if you're dating someone (or worse, married to someone) who likes to belittle you and destroy your confidence, you need to do some very serious thinking about the future of that relationship. *Both* of you are going to have to change if it's to stand any chance of surviving.

Negative thinking or useful criticism?

You need to be able to handle feedback from your friends. But you need to be able to distinguish what's real, useful advice and what's negative thinking.

Think about what people say: is it true? Is it honestly offered advice? And if so, is there something you can use to make your life better? For instance, "your temper is dreadful" --if you hear that from all your friends, it's probably true. Can you work on becoming calmer and less stressed? Would that make your life easier? Would it make you feel happier with yourself? Can you ask some of your friends to help you deal with the issue? If the answer to all those questions is "yes", then it's worth acting on the criticism.

On the other hand, a teacher you don't get on with may predict that you'll fail all your exams. That can be a real downer, but if you think about it, that teacher only takes you for one subject. So how would they know about your performance in the other subjects you're taking? Ask yourself why they're saying that you'll fail. You may, for instance, be the kind of student who asks a lot of questions--if they see that as you challenging their authority, they could feel threatened and angry.

Look for the useful part of a comment. "You'll fail your exams" isn't useful at all. "You'll fail your exams unless you do some serious revision" is partly useful if it's true. You now need to do the job of turning it into a positive. "I *will* do some serious revision, and I *will* pass my exams."

Ignore criticism unless it is constructive--unless it shows you a way to fix things. That doesn't mean you should surround yourself with yes-men.

Sometimes friends need to say, "Whoa! Back off there! That's really not a good thing to do!" And if they're good friends, you ought to listen--maybe they have a different perspective. Maybe they have experience or expertise that you don't. Maybe they think you have underestimated the importance and seriousness of a step you're about to take. But good friends will only say that kind of thing exceptionally. More often, they will support you, or ask you questions like "How are you going to get there? What time does the train go?" - that can help you refine and carry out your plans.

Good friends support each other. Recognize and value that support when your friends offer it; make sure you communicate your gratitude. And in turn, support *your* friends with constructive feedback, not negative thinking of your own.

Chapter 4 – A Sense of Self-Worth

Negative thinking often goes along with a low sense of self-worth or with low self-esteem. That causes real problems for many people in their lives. For instance, how do you present yourself confidently in your job if you don't *feel* confident? You may go along with things because you don't feel confident enough to protest that you're not happy with them, and then feel guilty because you went along with them, putting yourself in a negative spiral of feeling worse and worse about yourself.

So, you need to start thinking about yourself differently.

This isn't about looking at your educational certificates or your resume. It's not about what you've done with your life or what you've achieved in your career. It's not about the kind of narcissism that's always trying to make out you are the best or the most powerful or the highest achieving person in your peer group. It's not about what you've done. It's about who you are. It's about valuing yourself as a unique human individual, and feeling that this, on its own, gives you value and importance.

It's actually very important that you don't value yourself according to external yard sticks such as qualifications possessions or achievements. A study from the University of Michigan shows that college students who based their ideas of self- worth on external assessments--whether that was academic grades or the opinions of other students--reported more stress and other negative feelings then students with a feeling of self-worth. They were also far more likely to have problems with drugs or drinking or to have eating disorders.

Challenge that critical voice

Do you have a critical little voice inside that's always comparing you to other people? For instance, every time you look in the mirror do you compare yourself to a friend who you think is much prettier or better dressed? Would you be happy with your salary except for the fact that you think Maria in the corner office gets paid more than you for the same job?

One of the first big steps you can make on the way to improving your feelings about yourself is to challenge that little voice every time it makes itself heard. For instance, you can tell it that if your salary adequately reflects your contribution to your employer then it doesn't matter what anyone else gets paid. You can tell it that it doesn't matter what your friends look like--what matters is that *you* look great. Tell it to pipe down!

Understand the meaning of your life

We talked earlier about analyzing the negative beliefs that you have that are buried deep in your subconscious. But you probably also have some very positive beliefs. You may have beliefs about the meaning of your life and what you would like to do with it. For instance, you may be devoted to education as a positive force in people's lives. You may be a teacher who lives for the moment you see one of your students really begin to understand a difficult concept that you've explained. One baker in a small town sees one of his biggest career achievements as the fact that he has trained three award-winning apprentices. He's won a few prizes himself too, but he's particularly proud of the fact that he is so good at passing on his knowledge to the younger generation.

It's worth sitting down to think about what is meaningful to you. Maybe it's your creativity. That might be because you're a musician, or you might direct your creativity into house decoration or crafts. You might be a lead innovator in your workplace. If that's the case, then your sense of self-worth may depend on how you use your creativity. If you're feeling in a creative rut or if you move into a new job which doesn't allow you to innovate in any way, that could leave you feeling low. But if you have identified your core value of creativity, then you will know why and that will give you an idea what you can do about it.

Once you've identified your core values and beliefs you can judge your actions accordingly. You can decide to take part in activities that relate to your core values. You can use those beliefs as a touchstone when you're considering what action to take. For instance, one writer was considering moving to a small town. Among her questions to the realtor was what kind of artists and cultural life the town had. When she heard there were several textile artists working in an old barn, a writer's group at the local library, several book clubs, and a small art cinema, she knew this was the right place to move.

If you recognized some of the characteristics of Impostor Syndrome when we discussed it in the last chapter then you can really benefit from identifying your core beliefs. By referring back to those beliefs every time you face a decision, you will build a sense of your own integrity, and that's a really good antidote to Impostor Syndrome.

Knowing yourself

One of the injunctions written up at the great Greek temple of Delphi was "know yourself". That's actually one of the most important factors in arriving at a sense of self-worth.

Having a real sense of self-worth means not allowing other people to affect your sense of who you are. It means being happy with your own identity and understanding that others' views do not reduce your value or define your place in life. It's not necessarily easy to arrive at this positive feeling about yourself. But imagine how much better your life will be when one bad experience, one failed interview, or someone disliking your new hairstyle, no longer has the ability to make you feel bad about yourself.

So, let's start with an exercise. Let's pretend you're magically transported to a desert island. You have no books, no job, no family, no public image to maintain, you have nothing except yourself. So, now you're on the island, who are you? What is it that makes you, you? And now that your self is the only thing that you've got left, how does that make you feel?

If you're like many of us, that prospect makes you feel pretty scared.

But let's go a bit further now. If you're all that you've got left, then what have you got left that's still of value? Do some really hard thinking about this question over the course of a few days. You'll probably come up with some answers that are fairly superficial and others that go much deeper to the core of who you really are. Write them all down. Just keep thinking about them. As you think about these different responses, you will probably come to feel that some of them lack weight, almost as if they could just float away, while others sink deeply into your mind.

You might say for instance, "I'm resilient, I'm a survivor, and that makes me strong." Or you might say, "I'm a problem solver, I'm an innovator, I can always find something to do in any situation." A very lucky few people will also say, "I know I will always be happy even if I only have myself for company." Not many of us can say that, but the whole reason we're learning positive thinking is to try to get to that marvelous place.

This is a very important exercise, and it's not one you should try to get done quickly. Give it as much time as it needs. You could find you're thinking about it over a number of weeks or even months, and in fact, it's not a bad idea to come back to it every so often or even have it running in the back of your mind continually.

Another exercise you might try is to think about the times that you have been most fulfilled, that you have felt most passionate about what you were doing, that you felt really in the flow. When did you feel you were doing what you were always meant to do? What do those times have in common? What does that mean for you when you're thinking about deep down who you really are?

Keeping it real

Of course, knowing yourself isn't only knowing your good points. We all have weaknesses, and even if you're engaging in positive thinking, you need to take those into account at some point. But let's not think about these issues in negative terms, that is, as part of your character that you'll never be able to change. Let's think about them instead as challenges, as areas where you have some learning to do, or perhaps also as areas where you should be a little kinder to yourself.

Think whether there are areas where you struggle a bit or where your fear or anxiety holds you back. What can you do to make life easier for yourself? How can you get better at some of the things you find difficult? One student found it very difficult to concentrate. Simply putting some soft music on headphones really helped to cut out distractions. Writer Zadie Smith uses a software program called Freedom which stops her accessing the internet from her computer-

-again just cutting out distractions to make it easier to keep the creative juices flowing.

If you keep making the same mistake, you don't have to keep doing that in future. Think about how you can recognize that difficult situation next time it crops up. Think about how you can do things differently next time. That might be as simple as just saying, "Next time I feel myself getting panicky, I'm going to ask a friend for help. I'm going to explain how I'm feeling, and I'm going to do it before things get really bad, so that my friend's help can be effective."

Look what you're *not* doing there. You're *not* saying, I'm a flake," or " I always panic." You're saying, " I know sometimes I panic, but I can do something about it." *That* is positive thinking.

Be honest but be forgiving

Be honest with yourself. What bugs you about yourself? What do you really hate about yourself? Write it down. It might really look pretty awful, but write it down anyway. You might even feel guilty about feeling that way about yourself. Now that's interesting, isn't it? It shows you that you do understand feeling that way isn't really right.

Sometimes what you've written will relate to your frustration with the fact that, let's say, you feel like a bull in a china shop when it comes to social situations. You try to impress people, and you know that comes over all the wrong way. You're being very hard on yourself there. One journalist, who had real problems with depression, asked his psychoanalyst, "I see people walk into a room as if they belong there, and they seem to be able to talk to anybody. They have such confidence and poise. Where do they get it from?"

He was very surprised when his psychoanalyst told him that most people have exactly the same doubts and anxieties and lack of confidence that he was experiencing. He was even more surprised with the follow-up, which was that when they had met in a social situation the psychoanalyst could not see any of that lack of confidence showing. In fact, he said, the journalist had looked as if he was one of the most confident and self-assured people in the room.

So, remember that you are most likely your own hardest critic. You need to forgive yourself for **Being Human**. You need to forgive yourself for your mistakes.

Imagine you have a friend who is sometimes a bit embarrassing. They laugh too loudly, and sometimes they talk rather loudly when they get excited about things. But they're still a good friend. You put up with the loudness because you know how genuine they are, because they are always enthusiastic about things, and they have huge energy and a good heart.

Now imagine if you treated that friend the way you're beating yourself up. You wouldn't do that, would you? It would be a terrible way to treat them, and it would probably be the end of the friendship. And it would hurt them awfully too.

When it comes to your friends, I'm sure you know those annoying little things they do, and you take it in your stride. You take it in your stride because we're all human. As the poet said, " To err is human, to forgive divine," and most of us manage to forgive our friends for lots of little tiny inadequacies and annoying habits such as the occasional lateness. Lots of us have friends who mismanage their financial affairs, who can never get anywhere on time, who have terrible memories and can never remember appointments--or people's names. But we say, " They're only human!"

So, next time you find yourself feeling guilty or ashamed or hating yourself because you did that dumb thing again that you know you really hate, you need to remember that phrase and say, " Hey, I'm only human!"

You are being much harder on yourself than you would on anybody you care about. So, lighten up. Look again at that list of things you hate about yourself, but now, imagine you're looking at the few negative points about a really good friend, or a partner, someone you really care about. Think how small those negative points really are. Set against them the good qualities that you have. Try to become your own best friend. As you start to care about yourself more, and to care for yourself better, you'll see that those things you hate about yourself become smaller and smaller, and the things that you value in yourself will come to fill your mind instead.

Getting back up when you're feeling down

Remember that it's OK to feel what you're feeling. Everybody sometimes feels down. Everybody has to cope with grief and anger and fear. That's all part of what it is to be human. So, if you get angry, don't beat yourself up about it; everybody gets angry sometimes. OK, if you didn't control that anger very well, then you can think about what you could do differently next time. But don't feel guilty about having been angry in the first place. Forgive yourself your rage, just like you'd forgive a good friend who blew off steam and didn't really mean to have a go at you.

If you're feeling depressed, some people will try to make you feel that that's wrong. You should cheer up, they'll tell you. You should get a grip on yourself. Or you may feel that being depressed is a form of mental illness, so you feel that makes you in some way wrong or valueless because you're sick. Cut yourself some slack! Everyone feels miserable sometimes, and a very large number of people experience depression. Again, this is just part of being human. So, accept those feelings, and don't turn them into a way to feel bad about yourself.

Daily affirmations

Daily affirmations strike some people as one of the cheesiest manifestations of positive thinking. Perhaps you imagine Ron Burgundy repeating in his dressing room, "Every day in every way, I'm getting better and better," and that's really not for you.

That's a fair point. A lot of what we talked about is about understanding yourself and your core values as a way to learn to love yourself and care for yourself better. You're an individual, so just applying someone else's idea of positive thinking like a sticking plaster isn't going to work. You need to develop affirmations that are right for you as an individual. And sometimes what's right for you will change over time depending on your circumstances and depending on the progress you make in positive thinking.

You want to address affirmations to the areas that need the most work. For some people that may mean repeating to themselves something very simple: " I deserve to be happy. I deserve to be loved." At first, that might not feel completely genuine, especially if you're starting to challenge a core belief that was instilled in you in childhood that you are not a valuable or lovable person and don't deserve to be happy. But by repeating that affirmation, you're starting to challenge those old negative beliefs.

Sometimes an affirmation might help you get through a particular experience, a test, or an ordeal. "I'm going to take my driving test. I'm going to *pass* my driving test." Or perhaps for someone who is learning to swim although very afraid of the water, "Fish can swim--and so can I."

We'll talk more about affirmations later, and I *will* be giving you a list of ready-made affirmations that you can use as good examples, but if you don't see one that suits your particular situation, the best thing you can do is to tailor make your own. That way, it will suit you 100% and do the job that it's intended to do.

Who is the best person you can be?

A lot of negative thinking about ourselves and a lot of our difficulties in learning to love ourselves comes from the fact that we're always comparing ourselves to other people. We want to be the ideal person, the person who's good at absolutely everything, the person that everybody loves, the person who has no weak points at all. We want to be the winner at 100% of the time, or we think we are worthless.

Now you've invested some time in getting to know who you really are and understanding your own values and the meaning of your own individual life. You are not to be defined by reference to other people but only by reference to yourself and your own values.

So, the question is not how can you be better than someone else. The question is how can you be the best *you.* How can you become better at being yourself? How can you live *your* best life? In any situation, you want to be the best you can. Your personal best is important, even if it means you managed to run a marathon in 15 hours instead of 16.

Let me take a poignant example. Most people would not find it at all noteworthy or exceptional to manage to walk 100 yards. They wouldn't understand it if you came into a bar and bought everyone a drink because you just managed to do that.

But if you lost both legs in a car accident and just learned to walk again after years in a wheelchair or using new prosthetic legs, you would be so excited and happy. That might not be a big achievement for anyone else, but it would be for you.

So, when you look back on your day, don't think about whether it was a good day in terms of other people's opinions or in terms of what the ideal person would have made of the day. Think about whether you did the best that you could. Think about whether you made the right decisions for you personally. Did you accept challenges that could help you to grow personally? Or did you pass up learning opportunities because you felt stressed or anxious about them? Did you remember to ask for help when you needed it? Did you look after yourself properly? Do you feel you were true to yourself today?

That last question is often difficult to answer, particularly at first. But as you get to know yourself better, you'll find it's easier and easier. And eventually, you will find yourself facing situations knowing very clearly what is the right answer for you, and what is the right thing to do. You may even, if you're lucky, find that you have a little voice saying, "Go on, you know what you need to do." That's wonderful because that little voice may not speak very loudly, but when it does talk, all those negative voices--other people's opinions and your internal critic--can't get a word in edgeways.

Turning negatives into positives

I'm going to quote Bing Crosby here. That may be a little dated for some of you, but I think one of his songs get something really right when he advises that you should " accentuate the positive, eliminate the negative". (And if you're somewhat older or have a taste for 1940s music, you may remember not to mess with Mr. In-Between!)

So let's talk about turning your negatives into positives. There are always two ways of looking at things--in fact usually many more than just two. For instance, one software specialist wondered whether she was too old to apply for a job in an innovative startup whose CEO was 10 years younger than she was. A friend who understood the techniques of positive thinking encouraged her to re-frame her age as a positive.

● She'd already succeeded in her career. She didn't have anything to prove.

● She had very wide experience in the sector because she had worked for both smaller and larger firms in a number of different roles. A younger person would find it very difficult to show such broad experience.

● The young CEO might well appreciate having someone on the board who could act as a mentor with regard to some of the challenges of the role, such as dealing with investors.

The friend also advised her to look around the industry for examples of successful older employees. After all, it's a bit sad when someone feels their productive life is over at 38!

She might also have looked for resources. That's always a good way of dealing with turning a negative into a positive. For instance, an older employee might feel their skills are out of date. So, it's time to look for some resources, such as where to find professional development programs or even retrain for a new career. Thinking about skills positively, for instance, you might say that you have a very good grasp of the basic principles of the subject and how to apply it in practice. So, all you need is an update on some particular techniques or new applications. That doesn't require a huge change.

You might also consider resources in terms of networking, perhaps with headhunters in the sector, perhaps with other relatively-older employees, perhaps with consultants to see whether becoming self-employed might be a better career path. Once you start looking for resources, you are already doing something positive and leaving the negative behind.

Let's take another example--this time not a career situation but an ongoing feeling of powerlessness arising from early experiences. Suppose you were bullied at school. That led you to consider yourself weak and powerless. But there are other ways that you could start thinking about that experience which would enable you to put it in a more positive light.

You could say to yourself that you are strong because you stood up to the bullies. You could say that you are persistent, because despite the bullying, you finished your course, and you got your qualifications. You might even say that you were smart because they never got the last word. And if you didn't let them prevent you from following your own path in life, then you can be justifiably proud that you have succeeded in resisting pressure to let others determine who you could be.

Accepting compliments and positive feedback

One thing that negative thinking makes very difficult is graciously accepting compliments and positive feedback. We tend to self-denigrate or to brush off the compliment in some way, saying things like, "Oh it's just something I threw together," or " I suppose I just got lucky." We do that because we don't really believe we deserve the compliment.

Think for a moment how the person who gave you that compliment must feel. The idea was to make you feel good, and it doesn't seem to have worked. They must feel a little disappointed. Whereas if you just say "thank you," you've recognized that they're being nice to you, you've given them a little positive stroking, and you can both enjoy a little smile.

So how is that such a difficult thing to do?

It's only difficult because we allow negative thinking and a lack of self-love to affect the way we respond. By effectively destroying positive feedback and refusing compliments, we're able to retain the negative feelings about ourselves unchallenged. So, as well as hurting the person who gave you the compliment, you're also perpetuating your own negative feelings about yourself.

One thing you can do to change is to start giving compliments and positive feedback their full value. For instance, you're wearing new glasses and someone says, "I like those-they suit you! They're really trendy!" Think about that for a minute. First, those glasses are a success. But secondly, that person identifies you with being trendy, because trendy glasses are just what you should be wearing according to them. So that makes you a trendy person. If you normally feel a bit behind the trend or a bit frumpy, then recognize that just for once you're really fashionable. And if you've done it once, you can do it again! Welcome to your new life as a fashionista!

Some people are so bad at handling positive feedback that they will not even allow teachers to give it to them. A participant at a singing workshop was told by the teacher that she had "lovely top notes." "No, I don't!" she shot back. It wasn't till the teacher told her she had just sung a pitch-perfect top C that she was willing to believe it--and make progress that led to her changing her music major from piano to singing.

When you succeed, recognize your achievements. Allow yourself to luxuriate in the good feelings of success. Breathe in the good vibes--how much bigger and stronger does that make you feel? You may have had a little luck, and you may have had a little help from your friends, but don't let that stop you from enjoying every success that you have. Without your input, it wouldn't have happened.

You might try a little exercise. Sit down, take a clean sheet of paper, and record what you have achieved so far in your life. You are not allowed to put anything negative. You are not allowed to say, " I haven't achieved very much," or" I was a high school dropout." You're not allowed to compare yourself with anybody else. So, if your best school friend was a cheerleader, incredibly popular, and the class valedictorian, and blah blah blah blah blah--that has nothing to do with your achievements, so do not let it put them in the shade.

Be honest and be positive. You can put down splendid achievements that everyone will respect, whether that's brilliant grades, or running your own business, or bringing up four children on your own. But you can also put down things that you found particularly difficult or challenging. For instance, if you were very unfit but managed through sheer determination to prepare for and finish a half marathon, that's an incredible achievement. If you were very uncoordinated as a child but you managed to learn how to dance rumba, that's a great achievement for you. You might even put down very small things like overcoming your fear of spiders when there was one in the bathtub!

Really think hard about all those achievements. If someone gave you a compliment or positive feedback, if someone valued your help with a project or an event, if someone comes to you asking for advice--you can put all of those on the list. Those are all ways to demonstrate what a great human being you actually are.

Once the exercise is over, why don't you keep that sheet tucked away somewhere so that you can refer to it later on? If you're feeling down, it might give you a little positive stroking and inspiration to get on with things. This isn't just a one-time exercise, because as you grow in confidence, you're probably start thinking about your achievements differently. So, you might want to do it again in a few months' time or a few years' time and see how things have changed for you.

Self-care

Many of us are very bad at the daily task of self-care. Women particularly are often very good at looking after other people in their families, whether that may be children or aged parents, but they may be less good at looking after themselves. Everyone needs to be cared for, and you need to make sure that you look after yourself properly.

Spas and health clubs are very good at advertising based on this idea. Taking a bubble bath or having a massage is not what we're talking about here though. We're talking about looking after your self-esteem and looking after your integrity, and we're also talking about insuring the right balance between challenge and relaxation.

This is not about pampering or luxury; it's about giving yourself what you need to stay positive and to grow.

You do need to give yourself regular rewards. Choose things you enjoy and do more of them. It's not necessary to give yourself tasks to achieve. You're not like a parent demanding a good school report before handing out sweets. If you got through the day despite any difficulties it may have presented, then you have done well enough to deserve a reward.

But remember to take that reward seriously. In other words, don't just swallow a big bar of chocolate and say, "That was great!" Allow yourself the time to experience your reward properly. Here are just a few ideas how you can do that.

- Put together a bowl of homemade muesli with dried pineapple, pumpkin seeds, and granola and really enjoy eating it. Use all your senses--look at how pretty it is in the plate, taste the goodness, listen to the crunch...

- Spend five minutes playing with your cat or dog. Really look at how they jump, stretch, and chase--look at the enthusiasm in their eyes. Enjoy yourself properly.

- Take ten minutes to do a Zen doodle on a postcard. Let yourself relax into the curves you are drawing. Feel the enjoyment of completing coloring in a part of the design-- how good it feels when that last bit of clear space has been colored in! Let yourself get sucked into the activity and absorbed by it completely.

- Don't just take a hot shower and forget about it. Really experience the warmth, the gradual relaxation of your muscles, the steaminess of the air in the bathroom. Experience that shower to the full. It will do you so much more good!

Remember to allow yourself some down time. When we're at work or interacting with other people, much time is often dominated by expectations and fears. The boss expects us to deliver, our friends might expect us to amuse them, we might be afraid the two big speeches at the conference won't go down well, or just that we'll get to work late if the traffic is heavy. We are stressed every day, and some of us are stressed every minute of every day. We need down time. We need time in which we are not focusing on meeting someone's expectations or on thinking about the future.

But the kind of relaxation we need isn't just becoming a couch potato or being lazy. It's activity that pleases us and engages us 100% but without stressing us out. There's an interesting study in this regard--Mihaly Csizentmihalyi defined a 'flow activity' in 1991, and a flow activity is exactly the right kind relaxation to help us with positive thinking.

A flow activity is one that engages you 100 percent, one that absorbs you totally. It's the kind of activity which when you do it, you don't hear the phone ringing, you don't notice anything going on around you, because you're so absorbed in it. Because you're so absorbed in it, you don't retain any spare processing power for negative thinking or worrying. And the very fact that you're so absorbed means that you're enjoying it and really paying attention to experiencing it fully.

Another key concept for self-care is to take care of your energy. Everyone has times that they experience very low energy levels. At a time like that, it's difficult to get anything done; it's difficult even to get out of bed in the morning. But often, we allow our energy levels to get low without asking why that's happening. If you're feeling drained, find a way to energize yourself. Actors are particularly good at working with energy. For instance, actors will do warm-ups to make their bodies feel more responsive and energetic. They may also work with imagery to make themselves feel more powerful and more awake.

You may find certain kinds of activities take energy away from you while others give you more energy. The right activities are different for every individual, but some things many people find energizing are playing games, enjoying time with friends, taking a walk, or playing or listening to music. When you've found the right activities to give yourself that energy, then make sure that you do them on a regular basis. Set aside some time for these activities; don't just use them as a reaction to low energy levels.

Another thing that's very valuable is to set up a positive environment for yourself–a 'me space'. That might be a garden hut, a she-shed, a windowsill shrine, or a study. You might even just take over the bathroom one night a week for a candlelit soak in a scented bath. Whatever your 'me space' is, it's intended not as some kind of pampering, but as a place where you are free from other people's expectations and where you can just be yourself.

It's for you and for you alone; it doesn't have to be fashionable. If scented candles are your thing, fine - if your thing is a model train set or an old leather armchair with the stuffing falling out, that's also fine.

Marie Kondo and positive thinking

At this point, you may wonder what decluttering has to do with positive thinking. If you wanted a book on decluttering, you would have bought one. Of course, decluttering is not the same as positive thinking, but it can contribute to your progress in making your life more positive.

A cluttered workspace or house can represent a huge demand on your time and energy. If when you get home, the first thing you have to do is make space to put your handbag down, your house is getting in your way. If when you get to work, the first thing you have to do is deal with all those pieces of paper you left on your desk and try to find out what you are meant to be doing today, then your cluttered lifestyle is stopping you from achieving what you want to achieve, and it is stressing you out. So, decluttering can be a step on the way to freeing up your life, and in that way, it's useful to think about it while making the changes that you have already started.

Perhaps more important than physical and material decluttering, though, is decluttering your objectives and your life as a whole. For instance, you may be the kind of person who takes on too many projects, perhaps simply because you do not want to reject people's requests for help. You may need to learn to say no. You may have a rather scattered life, doing a lot of different things which don't really relate to each other because they all seemed like a good idea at the time. Do some thinking about which activities you really value, which are fun to do but not important, and which things you might give a miss entirely. You only have one life to live, so don't try to live 3 or 4 at a time!

Marie Kondo says that we should only keep those things which spark joy. Realistically, your work may not spark immense joy in you but it pays for the other things which do. But looking at whether the various projects and activities that you're engaged in spark joy is not a bad way to declutter your life. And once you've decluttered your life, you will be less stressed because you will have more time in which to focus on those joyful activities.

Self-compassion--or 'don't beat yourself up'

Many of us beat ourselves up every day for our faults. If we do something wrong, we hold on to it. We keep thinking about it and feeling guilty about it and allow it to make us feel that we are worthless or even faulty individuals. We may get angry or frustrated with ourselves. We start wallowing in negative thoughts and negative emotions.

It doesn't have to be like that.

Let's put the imagination to work again on our behalf. Can you imagine you have a baby? You have a very young baby who is, like all babies, having a hard time learning basic physical coordination.

Your baby has just gotten to the stage of trying to feed herself, and she hasn't quite got the right idea about how to hold the spoon. The food goes all over the floor, all over the walls, and all over you.

Your response to this will probably be to laugh. Babies do this kind of thing because they are very young, and they have a lot to learn. And you know that in a while, your baby will learn how to hold a spoon properly and how to put food in her mouth without getting it all over the room. So perhaps you might very gently take the spoon away from the baby and feed her yourself for the moment. Or you might put your hand around the baby's hand and help her to feed herself. But whatever you do, you will do it with gentleness and with love.

Now imagine that you have lost your temper with someone. Someone at work let you down, and you exploded. You are serious with yourself for losing your temper. You are frustrated--you know this is a problem, but you didn't see it happening. You didn't do anything to head it off until it was too late, and you were already shouting at your colleague. You are a horrible person, you say to yourself. You are an angry person, and you are uncontrolled, and there is something wrong with you... Recognize this? *You are beating yourself up.*

Why don't you try looking at yourself the same way you would look at that little baby? Look at yourself with compassion, gentleness, and love. "I've done something wrong. Sometimes, I don't do things very well. But I can learn to be better." True, it is taking you rather a long time to learn how to do it right. But then it takes babies years to learn how to use a knife and fork. So, give yourself that time.

Did your colleague storm out or demand you be sacked? Hopefully not. In which case, no harm done--you can apologize, and you can do better tomorrow. In fact, the work you have put into positive thinking and improving your knowledge and acceptance of yourself will probably show through in your apology. "I know I have a short temper," you can say, "and I'm working on it, but obviously it got the better of me." You might even ask your colleague to help in future - say by gently inviting you to take a break when it's clear you're getting frustrated. (One property broker gave all his colleagues a code word to use--"time for Oreos!" Whenever he's getting stressed, they remind him--and because they do it with humor and friendship, it works.)

Gently tell yourself that you can do better. Take yourself through how you might have approached the situation differently, just as if you are explaining to a young child how to do it. There is nothing wrong with you; you just got things wrong that one time. You have all your future ahead of you to learn and to improve.

Have you ever seen that kind of super-stressed parent at football matches who spends all their time yelling at their child? Telling him what to do, telling him he's useless, he's a wimp, he missed his chance, he's no use? You probably wince when you see that. How can that poor kid grow up to have any confidence? Or enjoy playing football? But many of us treat ourselves exactly the way those kinds of parents treat their children. How are we ever expected to get things right and enjoy our lives with all that screaming going on?

So. it's time to tell that bossy, stressed-out parent to shut up. Treat yourself instead like a nurturing, kindly uncle or auntie!

Sometimes we even beat ourselves up for feeling particular emotions. The logic goes like this: "I'm afraid. I shouldn't be afraid. Being afraid is for wusses. My being afraid means I'm a weak person." It's twisted logic which takes an emotion you feel in a particular situation, at a particular time, and makes it stand for your entire personality.

That can be particularly dangerous when you are learning positive thinking, because you may start to feel guilty about feeling negative emotions or thinking negative thoughts. Of course, that guilt is itself a negative thought, which comes with a lot of negative emotions attached.

Remember that you are human. You will feel grief, anger, sadness, doubt. Don't beat yourself up because "you're not being positive enough" or make the generalization that "you're just a miserable person". Recognize that emotion, and recognize that because you're human, you will feel emotions like this from time to time. And then move on.

The ancient Greek philosopher Heraclitus said that *'panta rhei'*, everything flows. Time moves on; things change; people change. In a week's time, the fact that you lost your temper today will have been forgotten by everyone. It will not matter anymore. So, it should not matter anymore to you either. Remember that things move on. Remember that tomorrow is another day. And be sure that when tomorrow comes, you can meet it with positivity and enjoyment.

Chapter 5 – Goal Setting and Permission to Fail

Many people who start positive thinking exercises do so with mixed feelings about the chances of success. They feel that there is altogether too much they need to do, that they need to transform their lives from complete failure into complete success. They feel that they have so many changes to make that they will never get it all done. They often feel of their lives in general that "it's all a bit too much".

One of the most important things you need to learn is to take things one step at a time. "How do you eat an elephant?" the old joke goes. "One bite at a time" is the answer. In order to eat your elephants one bite at a time, you need to learn how to set yourself goals that represent small and achievable steps on the way to your ultimate objective. Things won't change overnight, but the most important thing is to ensure that you are making many small but successful changes.

Imagine the sea eating away at the rocky coastline. If you were to visit that place for a week, you wouldn't see any difference at all. Maybe even if you were to visit at different times over a year, you wouldn't see any difference. But all the time, the sea is eating away, eroding the rock. Just one little particle at a time adds up, over time, to a massive amount of erosion. Eventually, maybe over tens or even hundreds of years, the sea will change the shape of the coast. Parts of the cliffs may slide into the sea. While the erosion was almost imperceptible when it started, it's final impact may be very dramatic indeed.

So, when you are setting your goals, think about small steps. You might divide a major objective into many small steps, each of which will get you closer to that ultimate objective. If you want to write a symphony but you haven't written down any music before, then perhaps a good first small step could be writing a short tune to play on your harmonica. If you want to become a millionaire, then your first step might be to develop a new product and put it on Kickstarter. In fact, that step would also probably be divided up into a series of smaller steps, such as identifying your target market, designing your product, making a prototype, trialing the prototype, and so on.

Don't aim too high but also don't aim too low. If you aim too low, you'll easily achieve the step, but it may not make a great contribution to your progress. And you'll also probably not feel that you have achieved very much. An effective goal is achievable, but it will take some work to achieve. An effective goal is also one that will make a demonstrable contribution to achieving that ultimate objective. And that will mean you'll be able to take some well-deserved pride in your achievement.

Let's take one example. A building contractor loved music but had been put off learning the violin at school by a teacher who was impatient with him. Aged 35, he decided to start learning again and was soon making good progress.

He decided that he wanted to play in public for the first time. However, he was feeling very stressed as he felt that he needed to play the piece perfectly; if he made a single mistake, he would fail. So perhaps he needed to formulate that goal a little differently. He could have restated his goal as "to play in public, and to enjoy playing", or "to convey the happiness of the music", or "to enjoy playing with other musicians". That would let him achieve the confidence-boosting step of playing in public, getting up on a stage and making music, and feeling good about it even if his performance had a few faults.

So often, it's instructive to think about how we treat children. A seven-year-old who's learning violin and plays at a school concert will get applause from everyone even if all the notes are wrong and she stops half way through to take another look at the music. That's because we want to encourage her. Sure, later on, the teacher will explain how to do better--but actually getting up there and playing took some courage, so we reward that. Treating ourselves like children is a great way to progress in positive thinking--and to achieve more in future.

Going back to the building contractor who is learning violin, let's look at how he should approach his relationship with other musicians. It would be very destructive for him to think about *competing* with other musicians.

If he's going in for a competition, for instance, then his goals should not include being better than someone else. You may find that surprising because, after all, it's a competition. But to get a benefit from playing in the competition, he needs to have a goal that is achievable and that does not depend on another person to make it happen. Winning depends on the jury or judges of that competition. It also depends on the absence, on that day, of a musician who is better, who has been studying longer, or who just happens to put in a marvelous performance.

But if he says "I want to play this piece the best I have ever played it", or "I want to really communicate the sadness of this piece of music to my audience", then he can achieve that goal whatever the result of the competition and whoever else is playing. And he is not comparing himself to someone else as a yardstick. He might even just say "I want to get through the piece without stopping," and that is not a bad goal for a musician who is playing for the first time in an examination or a competition setting.

Remember that you don't have to achieve your goals entirely on your own. In fact, looking for resources could be a goal in itself. You could consider training courses, friends, mentors, teachers, helpers, work colleagues who can be involved in the project. Those are all potential resources to help you meet your goals.

You should also remember that there is only one person who gets to choose your goals. Your boss can only give you an action point, but it's up to you to decide to take it on. If you remember, *Mission Impossible* always began with words " your mission (should you choose to accept it)". OK, most of the time you will accept exactly what your boss sets you in the way of a task, but think about whether you can ask for more help in achieving it or whether you could get some leeway on the milestones before you say " yes".

You get to choose whether you want to reach this goal or not. It's your goal, not someone else's, and it's you who determine when you have been successful. Recognizing that you have the responsibility for making that choice can be difficult, but it is extremely powerful. You and only you are in charge.

Recognizing your achievement

Buying this book indicates that you are dissatisfied with your life at the moment. You may want to fix all your problems at the same time. Realistically, that's not going to happen. Instead, you need to fix problems one at a time.

You will have many stages on the road from where you are now to a more positive lifestyle. You may start by challenging those negative beliefs that have been holding you back, but it will take you some time to make other changes. That's why recognizing your achievements when you succeed in meeting a goal is very important to your continuing motivation and your ultimate success.

63

So, every time that you fix a problem you need to recognize that achievement properly. Goal-setting is not just about creating improvement, but it's also about recognizing it. If you like, it is about "ticking off" that problem that you just fixed or that skill you just learned. That recognition--"I fixed a problem!"--gives you the motivation to move on up the ladder, to continue to achieve more of your goals, or simply to fix another problem. That creates a virtual circle in which every time you achieve one goal, it will give you a positive impetus toward the next.

Keeping a record of your achievements is not at all a bad idea. Write down your big objectives, break them down into short-term goals, and then tick them off when you have achieved them. Or even better than just ticking them off, use colored crayons or marker pens to color in the goals that you have achieved. Allow yourself to have a bit of fun. It may sound dumb, but engaging your imagination or sense of humor helps to embed those feelings of achievement deeper in your brain, making you feel more confident and at ease.

Gratitude journals

I've recommended writing things down a few times. It's a great exercise for keeping you on track. Gratitude journals are a special area where writing things down can really help you to maintain your positive attitude.

Different people have different practices. For instance, some people sit down at a regular time every evening and write three good things about their day. Others try to write each day about a different thing they are grateful for in their lives--that might be an inspirational teacher, a spouse, children, things they have learned, or even qualities that they are grateful they possess. Being grateful to yourself is a form of self-care and self-love, so that can be particularly powerful as an element in your gratitude journaling.

What kind of things might you be grateful for? Responses that people have made in their journals include:

- the music of Jimi Hendrix

- snowdrops coming up in the garden

- a friend's support during a difficult time

- inspiration from a teacher

- the cuteness of kittens

- just being alive

- a partner's love

As you can see, it's possible to be grateful for many different kinds of things from those that are important on the level of our lives as a whole to the incidents of daily life.

Journaling is easy to start, but it isn't the easiest thing to keep doing continuously. Many people start it and then break off initially for a day or two, but then they find they haven't done it for a week or longer. It can be much easier to keep to your gratitude journaling habit if you can fit it with another regular event such as your morning coffee break. You might work with other members of your family or with buddies to keep inspiring each other and make sure you're all on track.

You can also buy journals ready-made for gratitude journaling which include prompts that make your work much easier by directing your thoughts along a particular path. There's even a journal made for skeptics, which includes the prompt "Why I'm grateful today, more or less" along with a selection of amusing quotes.

By the way, if journaling. sounds a bit trendy or new age-y to you, you might be interested to find that a number of rigorous academic studies have found that it's beneficial to its practitioners. Benefits include a lower level of stress, better health, and a more positive attitude to life. It has been advocated by Robert Emmons, a psychology professor at the University of California-Davis, among other academics.

Permission to fail

While talking about goal setting and achieving your goals, it's important to remember to give yourself permission to fail. Of course, you won't give yourself permission to fail all the time! That would remove the whole point of setting goals! But failure is part of what makes us human, and it's important to accept that, from time to time, you will fail to achieve one of your goals. It's important, also, that you see that failure as a reflection of the fact that you are human, not as something that reduces your value as a human being.

It's particularly important to give yourself permission to fail when you are learning a new skill or technique. Failure is part of the learning process. If you're never prepared to fail, you will resist trying out new techniques. You'll resist innovation and adventure, and you won't learn anything new.

Research has shown that when learning a new language, students who are not prepared to make mistakes learn more slowly. Because they do not want to make mistakes, they speak less often and are less involved in the class than other students. On the other hand, students who are prepared to commit grammatical errors in order to engage in conversation tend to do better. After a while, their grammar will improve, and they will retain the advantage of having become more fluent in the language.

So, when you are setting goals for learning, it's important to concentrate on what learning points you want to achieve not on other outcomes. For instance, if you're attending a class on a new type of computer programming, your goal would be to learn the principals involved. You may end up designing a program that doesn't work. That doesn't matter, as long as you can see why it didn't work and as long as you learned from the experience. Perfection isn't necessary when you are in learning mode.

With life in general, it's always better to concentrate on the positive learning points from an experience rather than the things that went wrong. Even if you did not succeed in achieving your goal, or if you did not enjoy a particular experience, if you have learned something from it, then it hasn't been a waste of time. Think about what you have learned as a positive contribution to your future.

If you're the kind of person who over-commits, you may find you always have a 20% rate of failure in your life--20% of things on your list for the day didn't get done. You might want to rephrase things so that you can look at that as having gotten an 80% success rate. Of course, you might also want to think about whether you should cut down on your commitments. Or you might just be happy to have a very rich and diverse life and accept that an 80% success rate is pretty good.

Try to balance your learning experiences between those where you're challenged and stretched, and those where you expect to be successful and which deliver a confirmation of what you've learned. Always being challenged is stressful, and it could be difficult to keep motivated. Always finding things too easy can be boring and is likely to mean that you're not really engaging with the learning curve. You could probably achieve much more. Find the right balance, and you're giving yourself some hard challenges but having enough successes to keep motivated.

Considering your progress

Most people are very bad at considering their own progress. If you are controlled by negative thinking, you will probably take a negative attitude to your achievements. You may minimize the magnitude of what you have achieved, or you may remember the negative points from an experience rather than what you actually enjoyed about it. As part of making the shift to positive thinking, you will need to get better at considering your progress in a positive light.

Let memories of failure fade. Don't keep revisiting them. You can still learn the lessons from that failure rationally, for instance by knowing how to avoid a particular situation, but allow the emotions associated with it to fade into the distance.

On the other hand, when you have succeeded, or when you have learned something, create a positive memory. Tell positive stories about your experience to yourself--they will eventually create a new you. Remember what it felt like to hit a high note for the first time, or to get a 'bravo' when you played a piece. Remember what it felt like when people started laughing at your jokes.

Even if you only succeeded at a small part of a learning task, celebrate that success and replay it mentally. Suppose you actually finished your first 5k run, even if you came in last, forget the other runners and visualize yourself reaching the finish line.

Permission to succeed

It's important to allow yourself permission to fail, but it's equally important to allow yourself permission to succeed. Don't dismiss success as just luck. Don't minimize the effort you have put into your success or all the talent you have that was involved in it either.

Ask people for positive and constructive feedback. Negative thinkers often will either not ask for feedback, or they will ask " was it all right?" which isn't really going to elicit a useful response. Once you have started with positive thinking, you will be able to ask "what did you like about my contribution?" or " how could I do better?" Don't forget to claim credit where you're entitled to it. You don't have to be a braggart. You can simply say " yes I worked on that" or "I helped with the chapter on journaling."

Above all, don't get involved in the negative thinking vicious circle of not taking credit at the time, and then feeling everyone has taken advantage of you when they don't give you credit in future.

Remember to give yourself regular rewards for your success. Let yourself take pride in your successes, and when you have failures, look for the silver linings and the positive learning points that come out of them.

Chapter 6 – Imagery and Imagination - Your Allies

Imagery and fears

Imagery can be very potent as a way of tackling negative thoughts and emotions. Many sports players use visualization as a means of improving their performance. This is as true at the top level as it is of amateur sports players. Imagery is also used in many cognitive therapies to help overcome phobias, depression, and anxiety.

Visualization can have a huge impact--remember the proverb about a picture being worth 1000 words. In this chapter, we going to talk about how imagery and using your imagination can help you deliver positive changes in your life and help you eradicate negative thinking.

One problem many of us have with negative thinking is that negative thoughts often come attached to very strong negative emotions. That's why we need something strong like imagery to combat that negativity. If you adapt your thoughts but you can't shift those emotions, your positive thinking will only be skin deep. Imagination can really help to eradicate those negative emotions.

Top athletes often visualize a movement in their heads immediately before performing it; for instance, a slalom skier may visualize herself negotiating the slalom track while waiting for her turn. Tennis players visualize themselves executing a perfect ace or reaching to return a brilliant backhand. This does two things. First of all, it's a kind of internal practice or rehearsal that familiarizes players with the exact actions they will shortly be carrying out. But secondly, they are imagining themselves carrying out these actions with success, and that acts as a boost to the confidence. When you use imagery in this way, its effects are extremely powerful.

Inside and outside

When you use images, it's important to think about whether you are inside or outside the image. In the case of athletes, they are always inside the image; it's an image of themselves successfully competing. When you are inside an image, that makes it a very powerful image with a lot of impact on your thinking. When you are making a positive image, you should put yourself inside it.

Sometimes it's difficult to imagine yourself in the image. You might say " I can't imagine myself speaking to a live audience" because you are frightened of that situation. You might say " I can't imagine myself asking my boss for a raise" because deep down you don't feel you deserve the extra salary. The very fact that it's difficult to imagine yourself in that image can you show when negative thinking is limiting your opportunities or where you really lack confidence. Keep trying because as soon as you are able to imagine yourself in that situation, you have taken a big step forward to being able to do the thing that you're imagining.

On the other hand, keeping yourself *outside* an image can help to reduce the impact of that image. If particular upsetting or stressful images keep recurring in your mind, you can reduce their impact by ensuring that you remove yourself from the image. By doing so, you are distancing yourself from the emotions that the image evokes. You might also try gradually to shrink the image and to reduce its vibrancy and sharpness--quite literally letting it fade away. Let's take a closer look at ways of manipulating images to your advantage.

Manipulating images

There are other ways that you can manipulate mental imagery. For instance, you can imagine a visualization in close-up. That will give it far more impact. On the other hand, negative images should be imagined getting further and further away.

Suppose that you were angry and showed your temper when you were discussing something with your friends. You may be feeling upset and guilty, and that might lead to your replaying the situation in your head. If you can't just let it go, then one way of minimizing the impact of those metal replays is to try to imagine each one a little further away. Eventually the distressing episode will be happening to ant-sized people in the very far distance. It won't be nearly so distressing then.

You can manipulate imagery to refocus outside yourself. As we saw in an earlier chapter, when you are experiencing strong negative emotions, they can pull you inside yourself and stop you seeing the choices that are available to you. By using imagery, you can switch your focus and free yourself from the negative 'box'.

To make a positive image have greater impact, you can also manipulate it in the following ways:

● play it in vivid color. Bright colors make an image more memorable and powerful.

● Make it move. Moving images are much more powerful than static images.

● use more than one sense. When mental imagery is complemented by smell, for instance the smell of coffee or fresh bread or by sound, it will be much more powerful.

- make your imagery in three dimensions. You might even be able to imagine moving through a building or walking through a landscape.

Using imagery as part of your goal setting process

You can use imagery for many different purposes. You can use it to deal with an individual situation that has arisen. You can use it to practice a particular skill or action. But you can also use it as part of your goal setting and achievement program. When you have identified a particular goal, you can then visualize yourself achieving it. In the example of a player entering a violin competition, imagery might include the audience applauding or the player making marvelous music. The player could imagine how the fingers and the bow interact with the strings of the violin. For a nervous player or for someone with stage fright, just visualizing themselves confidently walking on stage could bring real benefits.

When you add imagery to your goals, you are not just enhancing your chance of achieving them. You are also significantly reducing your stress. Something you have already *imagined* hundreds of times will not be as scary as doing something for the first time--even though you haven't done it in reality before.

Using imagery can also help to crowd out anxiety and negative thoughts. If you are visualizing yourself successfully walking out onto that stage and smiling at the audience, you are not worrying about whether your hands will sweat, whether you will trip over the electric cable, whether you will miss your cue. You are concentrating on your success, and by doing so, you are ceasing to worry incessantly about what could go wrong.

More general uses of positive imagery

Studies have shown that even when people used positive images that didn't relate to their own goals or circumstances, thinking about positive images created a benefit. This actually means that if you spend half your morning looking at pictures of cute kittens on the internet, you will be less stressed and achieve all your goals at work. It's unfortunate that your boss probably won't believe that, but it is at least partly true!

Of course, what's positive imagery for one person might not do it for someone else. If you're a dog person, you may have groaned at the mention of pictures of cute kittens. You need to find the positive imagery that registers with you. That may be a peaceful landscape, it may be a picture of someone close to you, it might be an icon or an image of a Hindu god or a particularly intricate mathematical design.

Some business gurus and life coaches like to use what they call a "vision board" on which they put photos of the things they would like to have. It is undoubtedly very motivating to see photos of super yachts, fast cars, big houses, and the other appurtenances of the millionaire lifestyle. However, there is one problem with this style of imagery. Such images are not about the real you, and they are not about reducing your stress. They are about a completely external source of validation--money.

If you intend to change your life completely with positive thinking, then just wanting more money or a bigger house or a multimillion-dollar yacht won't take you all the way. You need imagery that allows you to feel powerful and valued in yourself.

There are now quite a number of guided imagery meditations available on the internet. Some are paid for and others, such as those on YouTube, are free. This can be a good way of getting started putting your imagination to use. Through guided imagery, you can learn to use images to affect your emotions, for instance to calm yourself down if you're feeling angry, or to instill confidence if you are feeling afraid. By linking particular images with particular states of emotion, you have created a powerful talisman. Next time you are feeling angry for instance, remembering your anti-rage imagery will automatically help you to feel calmer. It truly is like taking an amulet or an Aladdin's lamp out of your pocket and rubbing it--the effect is magical.

Anchoring

Anchoring takes the Talisman-like aspect of imagery a little farther. In anchoring, you evoke a time in your life when you felt confident, powerful, and at ease. You might evoke that with a single image. For instance, you might remember the time when your child brought you a little bird that had hurt itself, and you managed to heal it and let it fly away. You might just imagine those tiny hands gently holding the bird. And that could give you an immediate rush of positive emotions--love, gratitude, happiness--whenever you think of that image.

Anchoring takes a bit of practice. NLP (Neuro-linguistic Programming) practitioners use it a lot. The word "programming" there shows you what you're trying to do. You're trying to program your mind to make particular connections whenever you bring that image to mind. You will need to invest some time and effort in creating your anchors, but once you have done so, you will have a very powerful tool to use against negative thinking and emotions.

Safely experience the negative

You can even use a technique similar to the ones you used to manipulate imagery to defuse negative emotions. Remember that all of us do experience negative emotions because it's part of being human. Allow yourself to experience those negative emotions, savor them, and allow yourself to express them; it's probably best if you do that while you're alone rather than yelling at family or colleagues. But as you express the emotion, try to move from expressing it directly to describing what it is like. Describe to yourself the physical manifestations of that emotion such as sweaty palms or a fast heartbeat. Describe those physical manifestations. Try to step outside yourself, as it were, and describe them in a very scientific way. You might try to see yourself as a third party, as if you were standing the other side of the room. As you describe what's happening, can you feel your emotion slowly fading away? You should be becoming more in control moment by moment as you learn to stand outside the emotion.

This technique is quite safe to use as long as you remember that negative beliefs and emotions *can* be challenged. You might even want to make an image of your positive thoughts challenging and overcoming those negative emotions. What does it feel like when you stop being afraid?

Again, you may be feeling this is all a bit new age-y. But you should know that medical professionals often use techniques just like this to help patients manage pain and fear and improve their chances of successful convalescence. They wouldn't do that if it didn't work.

Children in hospitals are often introduced to imagery as a way of managing their pain and fear. Great Ormond Street Children's Hospital in London uses guided imagery to help children cope with painful medical procedures. For instance, a child may be asked to imagine climbing up 10 steps to get into the stands to watch a football match. Each of those steps will allow the child to enter a more relaxed state as the guided imagery works as a form of hypnotherapy.

Children who are very frightened may be asked to imagine a friend going through the procedures with them. They can be asked to help their friend by reassuring them and by telling them why those procedures need to be carried out. This form of imagery enables children to distance themselves a little from the medical procedure and from the very strong emotions that they feel about it.

It is a way of enabling them to experience those negative emotions in a safe way-- "I'm asking for a friend"--and in a way that will lend itself to progressively reducing them.

Shakespeare's Hamlet says that "there is nothing either good or bad but thinking makes it so." By changing our thinking about something, we can help to change its impact on our lives. Imagery is one of the best and most powerful ways we have of changing our thinking and changing our lives for the better.

Chapter 7 – The Virtuous Circle of Support, and Keeping on Track

Negative thinking embeds us in a negative spiral. We think things will be bad, then we behave in a way that makes things worse, and then we point to that as confirmation of a negative thinking. That's why it's so dangerous--and why positive thinking can make such a huge change for the better in your life.

Fortunately, once you've got started with positive thinking, there is a positive spiral or virtuous circle that works for us rather than against us. You start out thinking that things will work well for you, you are confident and behave in such a way as to achieve your goals, and once you've achieved those goals, you allow your success to confirm your positive thinking.

In this chapter, let's talk about another virtuous circle that can help you change your life. That's the virtuous circle of support. While much of the work of challenging negative thinking and becoming a positive thinker is work that you have to do on your own, you will be much more powerful with the support of your friends. And your friends will be much more powerful with your support too.

How to support your friends

When you start positive thinking, you will see many more opportunities to support your friends. You will be better able to support them as well, partly because you will be more confident and partly because you will understand the most appropriate way to offer your support.

For instance, if friends are feeling low, you can probably detect some of the negative thinking that's making them feel that way. You might be able to help them challenge that negative thinking. You probably realize that they are not feeling very powerful or confident, so you need to offer some support for their self-image. Saying something like "I know you will be able to cope; you are just the kind of person who can manage this sort of situation" may not be directly helpful in solving a practical problem but can give your friend some of the positive affirmation that they need.

If you are yourself more confident, you will not feel threatened by your friends' problems or by their successes. Your friends will be able to see that your help isn't motivated by your need to feel superior, simply by your friendship and desire for them to be happier and have a better life.

Asking what they need

Sometimes friends will not have the confidence to ask you for help, but you will have detected that something is wrong. In that case, you need to kick start the virtual circle of support by asking them if there's something upsetting them or if there's something that you can help them with. Even when friends do ask you for help, they may not be specific about what they want. In fact, they may not *know* exactly what they want! Often when people are emotionally upset or worried, they don't think very clearly about how other people can help them.

So, it's important that you know how to elicit exactly what help you can give. A general question, like "how can I help?" or "what would you like me to do?" might get the right response. But sometimes you might need to go further. You might need to have a guess at the negative beliefs that are causing your friends problems. You have worked through your own negative beliefs and successfully challenged them so help your friends to do the same.

Encouragement

Some people see their job as making sure that none of their friends think they're too special. They like to cut them down to size. They like to make sure that everyone conforms to group norms. If a friend talks about auditioning for Broadway, their immediate response will be to remind him that it's really difficult to get a part. That sounds as if they're really nasty people--but in fact, they may not even be aware of what they're doing or of the subconscious motivation behind it.

Now you've learned how positive thinking can transform your life, it's time to help transform your friends' lives too. When a friend is considering making a decision or trying out something new, try to support them and give them as much encouragement as you can.

You may not think their idea is necessarily the greatest. But rather than saying it's a terrible idea, try asking them questions to see if they've thought their way through the issues. For instance, "what kind of monologue are you going to use as your audition piece? How can you stand out from the crowd? Do you know exactly what the director is looking for in terms of age and acting style?" Those are all good questions which might help your friend prepare for the audition. (And if he already has all the answers, it will be interesting for you to find out more about the part!)

The praise sandwich

The praise sandwich is a great concept which can help you support your friends while letting you express your concerns at the same time. It's also particularly good for helping children and teenagers or students grow up to become confident individuals, as you take care to match every piece of feedback with an element of praise. In a way, it's like sugaring a pill. For instance, you could say "I really like the way you sang that song; it was very expressive. But perhaps you could make the second verse even softer, and then that would let you make a much bigger contrast when you go back to singing really loudly in the last verse."

You may need to find that to do this, you need to do a lot more thinking than usual before you open your mouth. That's quite normal. Not many of us are born diplomats, and tact isn't a quality that all of us possess by nature.

Some parents and teachers question the regular giving of praise to children. They think that it could spoil them and that it is often effusive and dishonest. While it would be wrong to deprive children of any praise because that's the beginning of teaching them negative thinking and could result in them having very low self-esteem, there is a nugget of truth in this. When you are giving praise, it is important to keep it real. Don't simulate something that you don't feel. Instead, look for some aspect that you can praise even when things have not gone right.

Sometimes the only thing you can say is that you understand what people were trying to do. They may have had good intentions, but it didn't work out. Or they may have simply not realized what effect their actions would have on other people. More often, you will be able to wholeheartedly praise at least one aspect of someone's performance or action, so make sure that you do that before you enter into any more critical feedback.

Remember that in any good relationship, it's important to remember why you are friends or partners--what you like about each other and why you enjoy spending time together. Sometimes, you might forget what your friends see in you. Your friends also might sometimes feel the same. They wonder why you hang out with them and don't feel as if they deserve your friendship. That's why it's important that you remind them why you're their friend. Recognize the little things they do for you, show that you value the fun you have together, or the fact that they challenge you and make you think more deeply about things.

And just as you should take time to care for yourself properly, you should take time to care for your relationships. Make time that you can share with friends and family. The same goes for your professional network. Make sure that you have some time available for colleagues who might need personal support. One investment manager is well known among colleagues as an excellent coach and mentor. She's always willing to spend 20 minutes or so going through a colleague's investment performance report to suggest ways in which that performance could be improved. That's not at all a bad reputation to have, and it means that she is never short of people to ask if she, in her turn, needs help.

Maybe right now you can't imagine yourself as a coach. Maybe right now you still feel that you don't have the expertise or experience or the confidence that you need to coach other people. However, once you have learned positive thinking and gained more confidence, it's a natural role to progress into.

Coping with the downside

Honesty between friends is a wonderful thing but sometimes criticism will hurt. Sometimes you will feel a friend has been unfair, and sometimes you know that the criticism is deserved, but it still doesn't feel all that great to receive it. You need to develop a number of mechanisms to cope with criticism.

You may feel angry if the criticism isn't warranted, or if you feel it hasn't been offered in a helpful spirit. If you're angry, don't immediately express that to the person involved. Instead, you could try writing a letter expressing what you feel. Then, *don't* send it. The letter has done its job in helping you get rid of your anger, so you can crumple it up and put it in the trash can.

If you simply feel hurt, you can offset that by thinking about what went well. Sometimes, we remember the negative criticism that a person offered us, but because our minds are habituated to negative thinking, we seem to forget the positive things that they said. Think back to what your friend actually said; what did they like or praise?

For instance, they may have said that your presentation was really well argued and delivered, but it was a pity the slides came out in the wrong order. Typically, you spend days obsessing about the fact that page three came after page four. How could you be so stupid? Why didn't you check before you gave the presentation? Instead, remember the praise--a really well-argued and well- delivered presentation! That's fantastic! As for the slides--you will remember to check next time. As you can see, the way you think about that presentation will determine how you think about yourself and your future chances of success. Don't skew your perception of feedback to the negative!

You can also make criticism work for you rather than against you. If a friend or colleague thinks you could have done better, you might consider asking them for coaching. You could say something like "I know that didn't work, so what can I do next time?" or you could accept their criticism and ask where you can find resources to help you do better. Do they know of a training course that you could go on or a book you could read that would explain a subject to you? Do they have a particular trick or knack to recommend?

Remember that negative emotions tend to close us off from the world and stop us from seeing the many options that are open to us. When you react with a negative emotion to criticism, you are closing off the ways in which you can use that criticism to learn and to improve your future performance. It's important to stay open so that you can benefit from criticism rather than letting it hurt you. The exercises that you did for staying open and freeing yourself from negative emotions will stand you in very good stead here. Instead of reacting defensively to criticism, you will be able to use it to your advantage.

Reacting defensively can also make your friends and colleagues feel anxious about offering you any feedback at all. It's a real pity if you close off that sort of feedback, as you are denying yourself useful information and learning opportunities. On the other hand, if you engage with the feedback that they offer and show a positive attitude, friends and colleagues will feel happy to offer you you feedback that you can use to improve not just your work performance but your entire life.

Above all, learn to forgive. The phrase "forgive and forget" is a little misleading because it suggests the two are the same. You don't need to forget to be able to forgive. You just need to be able to separate a criticism, whether justified or not, from the person offering it. Another way of saying that is, of course, " don't shoot the messenger!"

Keep in good company

One thing that all positive people will tell you is that they are surrounded by love. When you think positively, and you have learned to love yourself, you will radiate love to other people too. When you're learning to think positively, you need to make sure that you are surrounded by people who will support you. If you want to put this in a very selfish way, you could say that they are your resources!

Make sure that you keep in good company. You'll want to find good mentors. Most people think of mentors purely in a career perspective, but in fact, mentors can be a huge influence on your personal life as well. The same is true of teachers. If you look at really great teachers in school, they are the teachers who inspire their students, not just in terms of learning an academic subject but in terms of personal development. When you're looking for teachers or mentors in your studies or career, look for people who impress you personally, not just in terms of their technical abilities.

Choose your friends carefully. This isn't about snobbery or selfishness. It's not about picking your friends from the right social class, making sure all your friends are really smart, or excluding friends who don't belong to the right set. It's about making sure that your friends share your values. If you are a highly creative person and consider creativity the most important value in your life, then why do you have so many negative friends who pour scorn on what they call your pretensions? They may not be bad people, but they may not be the Right Friends for you. On the other hand, an artist can be very good friends with an accountant or an engineer if they share that desire to be creative--though they might express it very differently.

As you grow in confidence, you will expand your circle of acquaintances to include students and followers and other people that you have helped. You may not be able to imagine that right now, and that's fine, but remember that as you benefit personally from your new confidence and positive thinking, it's important to give something back.

Chapter 8 – Mindset habits and affirmations

Positive thinking is not magic; it's a matter of having good mental habits. Positive thinking is very similar to being a runner in that you'll need to do a certain amount of practice every day, and that practice will directly benefit your performance. Anyone who's targeting running a marathon will start running half an hour or more every day, and they will gradually increase their stamina and their speed. Once you get set on the positive thinking path, you'll be doing much the same. You will be making your mind fitter, just as a runner makes those muscles work better.

One of those good habits is turning negatives into positives. UK Prime Minister Mrs. Thatcher said of one of her ministers, Other people bring me problems; he brings me solutions." Whatever you think about her politics, she was very astute when she said that. Some people look at life as a series of problems, while other people see it as a huge ocean of opportunities.

You can even see your failures as learning opportunities. If you like, you are re-branding your failures! But it's not just a simple re-branding like slapping a new label on a bottle of beer. By looking at a failure as an opportunity to learn and to improve, you are doing two things. First of all, you are giving yourself more and more opportunities to improve, and by doing so, you will be able to improve quickly and more durably. But secondly, you are changing your mindset so that a failure will not knock you back and depress you. When you fail, you will not be despondent, but you will immediately start thinking how you can move on.

And of course, the other benefit is that you will not be tempted to use that failure as confirmation of low self-esteem. Many people allow every failure to reinforce a negative view of themselves. You can be different; instead, you can continue to be confident in your own abilities and to see any failure as just a temporary phenomenon. That's similar to the way you might see a thunderstorm. It's just a bit of bad weather happening at one particular time and in one particular place, but it doesn't mean the entire world is full of thunderstorms all the time.

There's a lovely quote from Irish writer, Samuel Beckett:

"Ever tried. Ever failed. No matter. Try again. Fail again. Fail Better."

Beckett is a writer that many people find slightly depressing, but there is a wonderfully humane humor in his works too. When you read " ever failed," you might easily think this is a negative idea. but the idea of failing *better* suggests that even if we are human and even if we never get things quite right, we can always improve. The idea that improvement is always possible, however many times we mess things up and however limited our abilities, is a very positive idea. Even if all we can do is fail, we can do it better and better!

Affirmations

We talked a little bit about affirmations in a previous chapter. Why do we need affirmations? Well, let's remember that inside many of us, there is that little negative voice that says things like "you can't" or "you're not good enough" or "you are really bad at this". We need affirmations that we can throw back at that internal critic--positive things that we can say to it to shut it up.

Affirmations should always be positive. Many people get this wrong when they start a diet or try to give up smoking, for instance. They make affirmations which are expressed as a negative, like " I will give up eating chocolate" or " I will stop smoking". Diets are often associated with negative words like hunger, limit, restrict, forbidden. That immediately makes you feel negative about the diet, and that makes you less likely to continue with it.

Instead, let's think about positive words that you could apply to a diet. For instance, you could use words that refer to the expected outcome rather than to the limitations on what you will eat. You could use words like healthy, fit, or energetic. Or you could think about the kind of food that you *are* going to eat, rather than the kind of food that you aren't going to eat. So, you would use words like green, tasty, and protein.

You could also use a vision board with pictures of the kind of food that's going to do you good. So, you could have some lovely pictures of salmon teriyaki, a really tasty-looking Caesar salad, and pictures of fresh fruit. That will help you to associate positive values with your diet instead of thinking about all those cupcakes and chocolate that you are not going to be eating.

Choose your affirmations to reflect your priorities. You know by now which affirmations you need the most. If you need to challenge a feeling of low self-worth, for instance, you'll need different affirmations from someone who is primarily concerned with overcoming a fear of flying. You might change affirmations after a while, and you might use several affirmations at any one time. The most important thing is to keep repeating the affirmations that you have chosen until they are a natural part of your thinking.

How can you ensure that you will repeat these affirmations? There are so many different good ways to do this. Write them on postcards, use them as your PC screen-saver, or put a post-it with your top affirmation on the steering wheel of your car so you *have* to read it before you drive to work. Record them on an MP3 you can play in the car or even write one on the top of each page in your diary so you'll see it first thing.

To be good, an affirmation first has to be relevant to you, and it also has to be something you want to say. You have to find it natural and pleasant to repeat. If you find it cheesy, it's not going to work. It's got to be *your* style. So, if you are naturally a skeptical kind of person, you will probably avoid spiritual affirmations like " I am one with the universe". Instead you might pick a punchy and realistic affirmation like "I am tough and strong" or " if people tell me lies, I will always find them out".

A good affirmation also needs to be pretty short. When affirmations get too long, they're difficult to remember, and that makes them difficult to learn by heart and repeat. If you're making up your own affirmations, you might need to polish them up a bit and condense them down to fewer words before they're ready to use.

So, with that in mind, here's a list of affirmations that you can use. Feel free to skim through the list. Some affirmations won't mean much to you, but you may find that your eye is immediately drawn to others and that you can see very quickly which ones speak truth to you. Remember you can always come back to this list in future at any time if you feel that you need different affirmations, whether that's because you've got tired of some of them, because circumstances have changed, or just because you have moved on.

250 affirmations:

1. I deserve to be happy. I deserve to be loved.

2. I am always learning how to be better.

3. If I don't get things right first time, that's okay.

4. I'm going to take the time I need to get things right.

5. I'm going to do my best. *My* best.

6. I am kind to myself.

7. I deserve respect.

8. I am strong and capable.

9. I have a lot to offer.

10. I am one with the Universe.

11. I have a genuine laugh.

12. When I smile, I make others smile too.

13. I'm going to be even more awesome tomorrow!

14. I work hard, and I know my value.

15. My heart is open. Love pours in and out.

16. I have many skills to offer.

17. I take pride in my work.

18. I am a creative person.

19. I am passionate about what I make and do.

20. I am always happy to share with people.

21. I am a loving friend.

22. I do things that I love.

23. My friends love and respect me.

24. My friends will make sure I'm always okay.

25. I'm stronger than I look.

26. I make sure my body gets what it needs.

27. I walk tall.

28. I'm allowed to have bad days.

29. I'm not afraid to be different.

30. I'm allowed to have a day off.

31. Life is tough, but I am tougher.

32. I am true to myself.

33. I let go of things I can't control.

34. I am a badass!

35. I have great inner strength.

36. I will take time to understand myself better.

37. I am a survivor.

38. I'm excited by what I can do with my life.

39. Let's remember how good today was!

40. I can feel at peace with myself.

41. I feel happy, and I want to share it with others.

42. There is no one else quite like me in the whole wide world.

43. I have so much potential.

44. I'm not sure where I'm going, but I know I'll find my way!

45. I am winner.

46. Things will work out for me in the end.

47. I can do this.

48. I can inspire other people.

49. I am fearless.

50. I can be patient. Good things come to those who wait.

51. I walk with elegance and poise.

52. I'm getting stronger every day.

53. No one can make me feel inferior.

54. My mind is worth taking care of properly.

55. I'm good enough!

56. I have the power to change my life.

57. I use my failures as stepping stones.

58. If I can't do a thing today, I'll do it tomorrow.

59. I'm not afraid to be wrong.

60. I have confidence in my skills.

61. I am an Explorer.

62. It's okay to say no.

63. I choose hope over fear.

64. I can complete every task that I begin.

65. I believe in the person I dream of becoming.

66. I don't have to take things personally.

67. I can choose what I want to do.

68. My opinion matters.

69. I am loved, and I am wanted.

70. I trust my own voice.

71. I choose my own integrity ahead of pleasing others.

72. I am safe.

73. I don't have to apologize for being me.

74. I will do what I set out to do.

75. I have set clear goals.

76. I can take responsibility for both failure and success.

77. I'm always growing.

78. I am focused.

79. I am persistent. I will never quit.

80. I will follow my dreams.

81. I can go with the flow.

82. I grab opportunities with both hands.

83. My comfort zone is always getting bigger.

84. I deserve the best.

85. Every experience I have will teach me something useful.

86. Every day, I will choose to feel good about myself.

87. When I love myself, it is easier to forgive others.

88. The more I give, the more I will receive.

89. My life is a big adventure.

90. I am wise.

91. I am my own best source of motivation.

92. I have great enthusiasm.

93. I have so much energy!

94. My power is immense.

95. There is no stopping me!

96. Today is going to be a really great day.

97. I'm so smart I could out-think Einstein!

98. I can fix anything.

99. I can let go of my mistakes.

100. I'm allowed to slow down.

101. I can be calm as a still pool.

102. Every day, I will move forward.

103. I will be a positive influence for others.

104. I am going to make everything work.

105. I am a problem-solver.

106. I will honor my own integrity.

107. I invest in myself--my skills and my happiness.

108. Positive energy surrounds me.

109. I am worth my wages.

110. Distractions cannot stop me.

111. Every day brings new opportunities.

112. My heart is open.

113. I love life.

114. I'm amazing.

115. Put one foot in front of another, and you can walk anywhere.

116. I am a never-failing source of ideas.

117. I am at ease with myself.

118. I'm on a mission, and I will succeed.

119. I can withstand difficulties.

120. I can change.

121. I can let go of the past.

122. I have a contribution to make.

123. I accept my power.

124. My mind and body are in perfect balance.

125. Every day, I start afresh.

126. I choose peace.

127. Yes! I choose to accept my mission!

128. I am unique.

129. My day begins and ends with joy.

130. I stand up for myself.

131. I am lovable.

132. My life is becoming richer every day.

133. I can do it if I put my mind to it.

134. I'm worthy of respect.

135. I'm open to adventure.

136. I take up the challenge of life.

137. By forgiving myself, I set myself free.

138. I will walk in the sunshine, and I will splash in the rain.

139. I speak with the voice of thunder.

140. I persevere.

141. I can organize myself and my life.

142. I am in charge.

143. I accept no limitations.

144. Every single day is a miracle.

145. Every day is a gift, and I will not waste it.

146. When I speak, I speak loving words.

147. I am special.

148. I love myself the way I am.

149. The world is full of opportunities.

150. I can learn from everything that happens to me.

151. I give Myself the time I need.

152. I have huge potential.

153. I am in charge of my life.

154. I will overcome.

155. I am big enough to forgive.

156. I can handle tough situations.

157. I deserve abundance.

158. Every step I take, however small, leads onwards.

159. I will let my light shine.

160. I'm perfect the way I am.

161. I can become who I want to be.

162. I can create marvelous things.

163. I can find hidden treasure within myself.

164. Every decision I make will be the right one for me.

165. I am an individual.

166. I'm allowed to take up space.

167. My past is over; my future opens up in front of me.

168. I'm grateful for my health.

169. I never do less than my best.

170. I can make a difference.

171. I can handle difficult people.

172. I can make today a great day.

173. I will not be afraid.

174. I am full of energy.

175. I am at peace with my past.

176. I turn heads wherever I go.

177. I inspire people to be their best.

178. I am surrounded by wonderful friends.

179. My work inspires me.

180. I am beautiful in my own way.

181. Even my weaknesses can make me strong.

182. Life will never get me down.

183. My thoughts are under my control.

184. I am faithful and loyal.

185. I don't need recognition from others, just myself.

186. I have the confidence to do what I need to do.

187. I am calm and relaxed in every situation.

188. I have an endless supply of tolerance.

189. I am always clear and focused.

190. I am a great learner.

191. I am a great teacher.

192. Yes, we can!

193. I am smart. I'm smarter than the people who say I'm not!

194. Fear will never get the better of me.

195. Every problem has a solution.

196. Every day, I greet the sunrise with a smile.

197. I spread blessings to everyone around me.

198. I create positive experiences for myself and others.

199. Every day gives me the chance to get better at being me.

200. Life is what I make of it.

201. I am positive and energetic.

202. I walk in strength and wisdom.

203. I will survive!

204. I am a magnet attracting all good things.

205. I set goals that I know I can reach.

206. I give myself permission to fail because I know that I will succeed.

207. I may not be fast, but I always finish the race.

208. I am indestructible.

209. I am open to all the opportunities life gives me.

210. I am a good listener.

211. My life is always unfolding in wonderful new ways.

212. I am brimming with energy.

213. I float above anger and negativity.

214. I become stronger every day.

215. I am filled with creative energy.

216. I am courageous.

217. People recognize my worth because I know who I am.

218. I abandon old habits for better ways to live.

219. I am a powerhouse.

220. I radiate charm and grace.

221. I am beautiful, inside and outside.

222. My life is just beginning--every day!

223. I am a great parent bringing up great kids.

224. My friends give me all the support I need.

225. I can make marvelous music.

226. My imagination is a source of strength.

227. My dreams are worth pursuing.

228. I will always follow my own path even if it's twisty.

229. I know where I am going.

230. When I speak, people will listen.

231. I can lead a team to glory.

232. I support people who need my help.

233. I know that I can always trust myself.

234. My life is filled with fun and friendship.

235. I am as free as a bird.

236. I am the way God made me.

237. I am a channel for positive energy.

238. I am abundantly joyful.

239. I have mastery over my life.

240. I can control my anger and learn to be calm.

241. I have the power to be completely serene.

242. I can break free of my fears.

243. I am relaxed and focused.

244. Every breath I take makes me more relaxed and calmer.

245. I accept myself and others the way we are.

246. I am open to friendship and love.

247. I release all negativity and tension to become free and open.

248. I give and receive freely.

249. I am a warrior for justice and truth.

and a personal favorite, which comes not from a self-help book, but from the science fiction TV series, *Babylon 5*:

250. We are star stuff. We are the universe made manifest.

Use your imagination to create positive self-images

Ditch self-deprecating humor. It's for losers. As soon as you say "oh look what a klutz I am" or tell a story against yourself, you start to believe it.

You can be modest without being self-deprecating. You can have humor without being a clown. So be careful when you find yourself making fun of yourself, and ask whether you need to take yourself a little more seriously and love yourself a bit more.

You may find that using mental images of yourself in a particular role can also help you affirm your own value. For instance, you might imagine yourself as a Maasai warrior, tall and powerful with your spear in your hand. You might imagine yourself in a stylishly-cut business suit standing up in front of an investor conference to sell your property project. (You might also imagine yourself as a bird flying free or as Michelangelo painting the Sistine Chapel ceiling--let your imagination soar!)

Sometimes our subconscious minds are a lot smarter than we are. A young man was trying to learn how to play the accordion. It's a difficult instrument because it requires coordinating one hand playing a keyboard with the other hand playing a series of buttons, and at the same time, you're using your arms to squeeze the bellows in and out. He couldn't get the hang of it even after a month's practice--not even to play a really simple tune.

Fortunately, his subconscious came to the rescue. One night, he had a dream in which he was playing the accordion perfectly. He was doing exactly the same things that he was doing when he practiced, or so he thought, but the most marvelous music came out. People were dancing to it and tapping their feet, and he just kept playing with no effort at all, really enjoying himself.

Next morning when he got up, he decided to try the accordion again. He didn't expect much to happen, but it had to be worth a go. To his great surprise, he was able to play--not perfectly perhaps, but a great deal better than he had been able to before.

Even more surprisingly, when he mentioned this to friends of his, quite a few of them reported having similar experiences. The mental images formed in the dream were strong enough to help him succeed in mastering the instrument.

A place of safety

A practice that can help with stress and feelings of vulnerability is to focus on images of a place of safety. For instance, you might imagine a secluded garden which fills you with feelings of calm, or you might imagine yourself at the top of a castle keep where you know no one can get in without your permission. One doctor who has worked in natural disaster areas and war zones simply imagines her favorite tatty old armchair when she feels the need for comfort and confidence.

Chapter 9 – Be the Best You Can Be

Many of us were taught at school to be highly competitive. Teachers would tell us to "be the best". Of course, that sets many of us up for disappointment when we realize that we are not going to be the world's greatest novelist, physicist, or entrepreneur. By definition, 99% of the class is going to fail to be "the best"; there's only one "number one".

A much more achievable task--and remember, a lot of positive thinking is simply about setting achievable goals--is to become the best that *you* can be. Another way of putting it is that you should manifest the best version of yourself.

To be the best that you can be, it's important to stop measuring yourself by someone else's yardstick. We talked a bit about having integrity--knowing what values are particularly important to you and making sure your life reflects those values. The only way to measure the best that you can be is to create your own yardstick. Comparing yourself to other people is never going to deliver the confirmation that you need.

Imagine a very, very fine young actor saying that he envies another actor. He envies her authenticity and honesty. He doesn't think he has that quality himself, and thinks he's too facile. That's David Tennant--who went on to become Doctor Who and play Hamlet for the Royal Shakespeare Company--about Anne Marie Duff. Using someone else as a yardstick is never going to give you useful information!

Inevitably you will be compared to other people, for instance through examinations or competitions, and it's certainly possible to learn from such comparisons. But the important thing is not to let the result affect your assessment of your own value. Don't keep matching yourself up against other people. If you do that, you will load yourself with stress, but you also miss much of the information value that a comparison can deliver.

We talked before about a musician setting goals for a competition he was playing in that didn't involve winning--enjoying himself or communicating the music's feeling, for instance. Let's think now about someone in a non-competitive setting. Suppose that you're learning guitar, and you hear a fantastic Jimi Hendrix lick. Let's look at the different thoughts you might have.

- "I'll never be able to play like that." Negative thinking! It may be true, but it doesn't help you. And who knows, maybe one day you *might* be able to play like that or at least pretty close. (Jimi Hendrix probably, when he first picked up a guitar, didn't think he was going to ever play like Jimi Hendrix.)

- "Wow, there's a lot of creativity there." That's a good way to approach Jimi Hendrix. Then you can think about how that creativity is shown. What does he do to the tune? How does he use chords to structure the lick? What kind of effects does he create? All the time you're formulating and answering those questions, you're learning. And your awe and admiration aren't spoiled by any negative feelings of jealousy or inadequacy.

- "What has he got there that I can use at my level of competence?" This is realistic but positive. Perhaps there's a particular vibrato that you can introduce to your playing. Perhaps there's a slide or a particular fingering that you want to learn.

As you can see you do not need to compare yourself on a level of 1 to 10 with Jimi Hendrix. You can learn from what Hendrix does without putting yourself down. Perhaps you could validly think about whether you can be as creative as Hendrix or whether you can take creative risks the way that he does. But in this case, you are not comparing yourself as if you are putting a value on your own ability; you are looking at the space that is available for you to grow into.

Let's take another example. Suppose you're in a music class with one class below you and one above. You *could* listen to the class above and think: "They're a lot better than me." Or you could listen to the students and say to yourself, "If I carry on, next year I'm going to be able to do all that!" Look at the gap as your potential --as your next goal.

Above all, you need to see yourself as a work in progress. Negative thinking encourages us to see ourselves as something that is not going to develop any further. Positive thinking on the other hand enables us to consider our future potential for learning and developing. Positive thinking is dynamic.

A good way to look at development is to set up your own yardsticks using your past experience. You could ask the question, " How far have I come?"

So, for instance, if you are getting started with music, you could take a recording of yourself playing a song. Then, in a month's time, you could go back and listen to it and compare it with the way you are now playing. You can see where you have improved. You can see how your understanding of the music has changed. Make another recording, and you will be able to go back to that one intern in another month's time. Because you are always recording your progress, you have an objective touchstone. If, at some point, you get discouraged and think you're not learning or progressing, you can go back to the recordings and see exactly what progress you have made.

I've chosen music because most of us listen to it even if not everyone plays music. Of course, the same applies to accountancy, to painting, to computer programming, or designing video games or brain surgery or using a CNC lathe. But I suspect most of us have rather less familiarity with those subjects.

By concentrating on your own progress and comparing yourself now with yourself a little while ago rather than with other people, you are supporting your positive thinking habit. And you can also establish a trajectory. Compare your position now with your position a month ago, and you can draw a line showing how fast you are learning, how quickly you are improving. Now if you want to, you can project that line into the future. That enables you not just to set goals for your future progress, but also to have full confidence that they will be achievable.

Slipping back? Don't worry!

Whenever we are learning, there will be times that things don't work out. We've already talked about how important it is to give yourself permission to fail. Often when we are concentrating on one thing, other things start to slip.

Every actor knows the string bag syndrome, though they don't all call it by that name. When you try to patch a hole in a string bag, you know that another hole will open up somewhere else. So for instance, when you're concentrating on the blocking--how the actors move around the stage--you're going to start forgetting your lines.

And when you concentrate on your lines, guess what, you're going to start forgetting the blocking!

The important thing here is to accept that this happens. Don't let it dislodge your positive thinking. Slipping back is not a sign that you have forgotten everything, and it doesn't mean that you're not making progress. Try to keep in mind the fact that you are making progress overall. When you are climbing a mountain, sometimes you have to descend to pass a gully or a small valley. That doesn't mean you won't reach the summit. It's just a step on the path.

A good way of neutralizing the string bag syndrome can be to concentrate very single-mindedly on just one aspect of what you're doing. For instance, if you have difficulty with one passage in a piece of music that you're practicing, you might just practice that single passage on its own. Play it in different rhythms, play it at different speeds, break it up into smaller pieces and practice those, practice until you have got that one piece absolutely right. That way you are not letting your frustration with that one small part of the task affect your performance of the rest of the music. (Have you ever listened to a student playing a piece when they know there's a really difficult bit coming up? You can always tell! They get tense, and suddenly the music isn't fun anymore...)

In the same way, you might be struggling with trying to integrate positive thinking into your entire life both at home and at work. Perhaps there's just one thing that seems to be stopping you making progress. Rather than let that derail your entire life, you should think about how to deal with that one issue in isolation. Accept that while you're dealing with it, some of the other issues will be put on hold and might even see a little slippage. But remember that those little slip-backs are strategic. Give yourself permission for those things to slide; don't feel guilty when they do.

You might think of yourself as a great military strategist. If you want to win the battle, sometimes you need to make a strategic retreat on one wing! Or you can find other images which will help you fight against the negative thinking that tries to turn every small slip into a disaster. Remember how powerful imagery is in helping us keep our minds on the positive thinking path.

Remember you need to Love Yourself

We have come a long way from talking about getting rid of your initial negative thinking. But it's worth remembering that you cannot be the best you can be if you don't love yourself. If you consider yourself an embarrassing or worthless human being, how can you ever discover your true self? How can you ever become the best that you can be?

The problem for many people is that they have accepted other people's agendas. Rather than becoming your best self, you will try to become someone else. You will try to become the nice little girl that your mother wanted you to be, the tough guy that your school encouraged you to become, the smart person your teachers wanted to see you as, but you will have left your real self behind. It's only by learning to accept and love yourself that you'll be able to create a sure foundation for becoming the best that you can be.

Chapter 10 – The Spiritual Value of Positive Thinking

If you are a skeptical type of person, you may have made quite a big stretch to pick this book up in the first place. When you saw the title of this chapter you may have been very tempted to put it down.

Please don't! We're going to talk about the spiritual value of positive thinking, but that doesn't mean we're proposing any kind of religion or trying to convert you in any way. We're simply using the word spiritual to indicate a deeper dimension to the practice of positive thinking.

Self-love

Self-love is one of the basic concepts of positive thinking; you need to Love Yourself the Way You Are. Many Buddhists would say, instead, that you need to have self-compassion; that's a way you might find more comfortable to think about this concept.

Having compassion for all living creatures is a central Buddhist value, but it is normally expressed as compassion for other living creatures. However, having compassion on your own self is also important. The Venerable Amy Miller, a Buddhist thinker in the

Tibetan Mahayana tradition, sometimes says "Don't beat yourself up!"

For instance, at a lecture to the Root Institute at Bodh Gaya, she spoke about the difficulties of maintaining a meditation practice. Many people start well, for instance, taking a retreat for a week or two, but when they return to the ordinary world, they find it difficult to continue regularly. The message "don't beat yourself up" is a great help to them, for several reasons:

> • You only managed to meditate for five minutes, not two hours? "Don't beat yourself up!" You still managed five minutes, and it will still do you good. Maybe you can do more another day.

> • You didn't meditate today? That must mean the end of your Buddhist life; you've ruined it. You'll never be a good Buddhist now. (Do you recognize the catastrophizing going on there?) "Don't beat yourself up!" Tomorrow, it's a fresh morning and you can restart and do your meditation, and you've lost a single day, that's all.

> • Meditation is intended to free the mind from worries and incessantly recurring thoughts. But if you are beating yourself up for missing a meditation session, your thoughts will keep going back to that subject, and you will be unable to free your mind.

Amy spoke about one Retreat she took during which she couldn't stop thinking about pizza. It was a fasting retreat, which made it worse! Rather than continue to obsess about the pizza, or rather the absence of pizza, she decided to imagine that pizza as richly and fully as she could. She took her time to imagine how hot the pizza was straight out of the oven, how good it smelled, how good it tasted. She actually ate that pizza in her meditation. And as soon as she had done that, the pizza stopped bugging her. The obsession was gone, and she could now meditate properly. By having compassion on her hungry thoughts instead of beating herself up for being distracted from the meditation, she was able to get back on track.

Meditation

You don't have to be a Buddhist to find meditation useful. In fact, almost all religions use meditation. Orthodox Christianity has a meditative tradition; Jewish Kabbalah followers meditate, as do Sufi Muslims and many Hindus. Plenty of agnostics and atheists also find meditation useful for clearing the mind, relaxing, and keeping themselves open to life and its endless potential.

A meditation is essentially very simple. Probably the simplest form is pranayama, in which you concentrate on your breath in order to focus the mind. Other forms of meditation use chants or mantras, such as "Om" or the name of Jesus, and some also use imagery as a focus. Although such sounds and images often have religious significance, you could meditate on the name of the Dude or the flying spaghetti monster if you wanted to, and if you did so with single-minded focus, that meditation would work just as effectively as any other.

If you want to meditate, one of your best resources is YouTube. You can download an impressive number of guided meditations for free. There are also apps you can download on your tablet or smartphone, such as Headspace and Smiling Mind. Or you could always go to a meditation class that's provided through a local yoga center, Buddhist temple, or education program.

Finding meaning in life

Positive thinking is about finding meaning in your life. Again, that doesn't have to be religious. It *could* be religious, and for many people it is, but it doesn't need to be.

A few examples of how people have found meaning in their lives show how they have created their own values and lived up to them. These people are not conventionally religious, but they have found a deeper meaning to the way they live their lives, and in doing so, they have also found happiness.

- "I've saved all my little cat family from the pound. They came as anxious, frightened, fierce felines, and now they are all happy, relaxed cats who know that they are loved. When life is getting me down, I look at my cats and I think, I've achieved something worthwhile."

- "I renovated this old watermill all on my own. I've saved something of our local history and I'm passing it on to the next generation. And I've got local kids enthusiastic about preserving our water-meadows. Every time I see a child smile at a frog jumping into the water, I feel great."

- "I just love painting, and I've organized my life so I can spend all the time I want at my easel. Every day I try a new way of putting my ideas on canvas, a new way of seeing the world. Every day, the world is worth seeing."

- "I've built a successful real estate business that's well respected. I know this little corner of the city better than anyone else; I've sold some houses twice or three times over the years! And I still love seeing new houses being built. I can't imagine a better way to live my life."

Like attracts like

Many hermetic traditions are based on the idea of like attracting like. At its simplest, that's how sympathetic magic works--the idea for instance that rubbing a lucky coin can attract money towards you.

I'm not proposing you carry out magic rituals as part of your positive thinking practice! But many people who have started on the positive thinking path have found in their own lives, and believe very strongly, that positive energy attracts positive energy.

If you think about it, that's not such a dumb idea. For instance, if you are in a room with a number of other people but just one of those people is full of enthusiasm and energy, that's probably the person that you want to talk to. In business, a confident presentation is always more convincing than an argument made by someone who appears more downbeat or hesitant.

Of course, that energy needs to be genuine. We've all experienced the kind of fake enthusiasm from the Charles Atlas School of self-help that says "Have a nice day" or "Wow, that's awesome," but doesn't actually mean it. What I'm talking about here is the energy that comes from positive thinking, that comes from being the best you can be and living your life to the fullest. We can all tell the difference between the salesperson who just wants to sell a product and a salesperson who really believes the product is great--that's the kind of positive energy that I'm talking about here.

So, on a superficial level, you can already see that like attracts like. People whose positive thinking has transformed their lives will find other people like themselves. That may mean you can attract a fantastic mentor, it may give you access to teaching programs you'd never get on otherwise, it may lead to profitable business contacts. Or it may simply mean that in a year's time, you'll look at your contacts list on Gmail and find it's full of fantastic people with great energy that you really enjoy hanging out with.

Some people take this idea of positive energy further. They look at the energy of the entire universe. There is such a huge amount of energy in the universe, and you have access to all of it to draw on for your daily needs. They believe that your positive attitude can actually bring good fortune; your own positive energy will attract wealth, health, and other good things. Certainly, the scientific studies that have been carried out on positive thinking do appear to show that as far as health is concerned, positive energy tends to have a beneficial effect on your life. Whether it will make you richer? The jury's still out on that.

You might also think about what happens when we introduce positive energy into the political arena. Very often, political battles are fought by using a negative mission statement--things that we *don't* want to happen. Such battles are often acrimonious, and they sap our energy, they don't put much back into our communities. On the other hand, when a political campaign has a positive purpose to make people's lives better or to improve a whole community, that can really energize people and bring them together. Whichever party you support, why not think about how to make politics a more positive space to achieve more for everyone?

Conclusion

Throughout this book, we've tried to give real life examples how you can apply positive thinking to your life. We started out looking at how to challenge and overcome negative thoughts and beliefs. Then we moved onto using positive thinking to create self-acceptance, self-love, and the opportunity for personal development.

If you've read the entire book, then you have an excellent basis for making positive changes to your life. Remember that adopting positive thinking is a long process. While you should achieve dramatic changes to your well-being in a very short time, the full benefits of positive thinking will accrue over the long-term.

You should find that life is significantly less stressful. That on its own should help you make other positive changes. For instance, if you're trying to give up smoking, that will become very much easier if you don't feel stressed out all the time. It will also become easier when you feel better about yourself. Some people who try to give up smoking fail because ultimately, they don't feel that they are worth the considerable investment in breaking the habit. Their lack of self-worth makes it impossible for them to make the change. On the other hand, once you value yourself, you can clearly see that you are worth investing the effort to make your life healthier and better.

In the same way, some people have a self-image of "that fat child" that started at school. They don't stick to their diets because somewhere deep inside, they feel that they have to stay fat. If they get thin, they will be someone else. That can be quite threatening. Challenging that self-image and getting a better feeling of self-worth has to happen before they'll be able to stick to that diet.

Positive thinking will transform your life, but it can also transform the lives of people close to you--your family, friends and colleagues. They may simply notice that you are in a better temper most of the time. They may find that you have new enthusiasm, and that may inspire them. You may find yourself for the first time being the person who proposes an outing or event, rather than simply going along with what other people have arranged. As your personal development continues, you may even end up taking on a leadership role and mentoring or coaching some of your colleagues. That might seem far away at the moment, but it's certainly something that many people who have adopted a positive thinking attitude have found works for them.

Positive thinking is also about looking at life in general as a huge opportunity--a vast storehouse of potential from which you can take freely. You will get better and better at looking for the right resources, whether that's finding someone to teach you how to fix your broken computer, or finding a local meditation group, or working out how you can finance a new business. While positive thinking starts by putting more value on yourself and learning to care for yourself better, you can leverage that impact by adding more and more resources, by learning more, and by asking for more.

I won't say the potential is unlimited. The most positive thinking in the world probably won't get you a gold medal for slalom skiing in the next Winter Olympics. It probably won't get you into the

White House either. But the changes you can make to your life with positive thinking are tremendous. Above all, whatever job you end up doing and wherever you end up living, with positive thinking, you will learn how to be happy and contented--and being happy is really the best thing you can possibly be.

Part 2: Self-Esteem

The Ultimate Guide to Increasing Your Self-Worth and Confidence Using Positive Thinking, Daily Habits, Affirmations, and Mindfulness Meditation

Introduction

We often talk or hear about self-esteem, but many of us don't really have a good understanding of what it means, how it is developed, and how one can cultivate it. Psychologists have long been interested in figuring out how and why people develop self-esteem, feelings of self-worth, and how this affects their overall lives and wellbeing. If most of us look closely at our lives, we can see how self-esteem, or a lack of it, has played a profound role in how we become who we are.

There is much evidence to support the notion that people with healthy levels of self-esteem function better in life, reporting higher degrees of personal and work satisfaction than those with lower self-esteem. While there is a lot of evidence suggesting that much of our feelings of self-worth are ingrained in us from our experiences, this doesn't mean we cannot make changes.

This guide discusses what self-esteem is, its importance, and factors that contribute to how we feel about ourselves. Once we have laid this groundwork, we will look at ways you can take control of your life and feel better about yourself and your prospects. It is a long, hard road for many, but the process of self-knowledge is highly rewarding and can have dramatic results in our daily lives.

We look at different ways to take control of our lives, thoughts, and feelings. We talk about the importance of self-awareness and self-acceptance, and taking responsibility for our thoughts and subsequent actions. None of this is easy and will not produce changes overnight, but with conscious effort, one can improve their response to emotional stimuli, learn to love themselves, and to gain more confidence about their abilities and potential in this world.

The advice we present in this book is backed by scientific rigor, and real-world testing, that has shown its effectiveness. Lacking positive self-esteem and feelings of self-worth develop because of experience over time, and thus, one cannot expect that it can be remedied overnight. It will be a long process and one that will probably have setbacks, but the ultimate end is more self-acceptance and self-love that will help you achieve what you want in life and give what you offer to the world.

Chapter 1: What Is Self-Esteem?

We often equate self-esteem with feelings about self-worth and the amount of respect we have for ourselves, including how we treat our bodies and mind. The dictionary defines self-esteem as "confidence in one's own worth or abilities; self-respect." This is a good definition, but the meanings of other words might need to be fleshed out. Confidence refers to how well we think we stack up against other people and how much weight we put behind our own thoughts, feelings, and ideas.

Worth is a bit harder. There are people who know they are good at certain things but still don't feel like they are worthy of respect and love, which many psychologists equate to low self-esteem. Abilities can also be tricky since they don't necessarily correlate with reality, which we will touch on below.

There are incredibly confident and resilient, who considerably overestimate their skill or talent. Finally, self-respect is another term we need to look at a bit more closely.

Many people would link self-respect with feelings of being worthy of love and, well, respect, but when looking at self-respect as it relates to self-esteem, we must look at the action. We can *say* we have self-respect all we want, but if we never concern ourselves with self-care and meeting our basic needs it won't make it true.

Just with the definition alone, we see how tricky it is to pin down what self-esteem is, which is part of what makes psychology, in general, a difficult area of science. So many of these concepts are subjective, and what we report may not coordinate with reality.

At first blush, most of us would probably think we have a healthy level of self-esteem, but upon probing deeper, we find there is a lot about ourselves that we haven't learned how to accept. Subsequently, this can have negative effects on our behavior and our lives.

Many people correlate high self-esteem with success. Although there can be a strong correlation between the two, *correlation does not equal causation.* There may be a relationship between the two, but that doesn't mean that one causes the other. More research needs to be done, and this is a difficult topic to get solid research data on.

Low self-esteem can undoubtedly cause issues. People with low self-esteem are more likely to have poor interpersonal relationships, find their careers lacking, and give themselves improper self-care. It should also be mentioned that excessive levels of self-esteem, what we most often call *arrogance,* can also cause problems. People overconfident to the point of arrogance often have issues with their interpersonal relationships and are prone to conflict. Either extreme is not a good thing. Like with so many things in life, the goal is to find the right balance.

So, it is clear that both low and excessive levels of self-esteem pose problems, meaning we want to fall somewhere in the middle. We need to accept and value ourselves enough we care for our basic needs and know how to ask for what we need in life, but we don't want to take this to such an extreme we see ourselves as more valuable than others and seek to dominate rather than cohabitate with others.

The Benefits of Self-Esteem and the Pitfalls of Lacking

People with low self-esteem often feel like a proverbial "doormat" because people walk all over them, and they feel as if they have little to no control over their lives. For people who lack self-esteem, positive feedback may be hard to handle. We all know that person that, when given a compliment, argues that it isn't true.

Excessive fear of failure is common in people with low self-esteem, and that often means they never try things that could lead to failure, even when it is something the person would love or be very good at. People with low self-esteem often talk about a lot of missed opportunities in their life. Roads are not traveled, and risks are not taken due to fear of failing along the way.

The amount of self-esteem you have can play a dramatic role in the success or lack thereof one's experiences in life. Someone's level of self-esteem can inform the risks they take in their life, the goals they choose to (or not choose to) pursue, such as better education and career opportunities. It can also affect expectations regarding interpersonal relationships.

Healthy levels of self-esteem allow you to see and accept your strengths and your weaknesses. It helps you express yourself to others, tell them how you feel, and know how to ask for what you need. People with healthy levels of self-esteem can take a compliment, but they can also take and grow from negative feedback.

People with adequate self-esteem have a good understanding of their abilities and know when to take risks. Taking risks can help build confidence from the success we see from the risks and what we learn with the failures we will experience along the way.

For many, their sense of self-worth and value is directly tied to self-esteem. If one doesn't feel good about oneself, they likely don't place a ton of value on themselves either. The sad thing is this is often expressed in poor self-care. Self-worth refers to the beliefs you hold about yourself, your abilities, and your value to the world.

Psychologists think of self-worth as a trait largely stable and enduring. That doesn't mean it cannot change, but it does show it is more difficult to break an ingrained trait.

What Effects Self-Esteem?

Abraham Maslow was an influential psychologist who developed a hierarchy of human needs. He theorized that self-esteem could profoundly affect our ability to meet our needs. He posits that both self-respect and respect from others is vital to meeting our needs. We cannot reach self-actualization, the highest level of his hierarchy, without both things.

A lot of things can affect self-esteem, from personal disposition, disability, and even genetics, though much more research needs to be done to understand this potential connection.

Life experience seems to be the most important factor in determining someone's level of self-esteem. People who rarely receive positive feedback or reassurance are more likely to have lower levels of self-esteem.

Signs of Low Self-Esteem

- The feeling that most people are better or more worthy than oneself
- Struggling to say no or to express needs and feelings
- Little to no confidence in one's skills and abilities
- A tendency to look at life negatively

- High levels of feelings of shame, embarrassment, pessimism, and fear of failure

- Feeling the needs of others supersede your own

Signs of Healthy Self-Esteem

- Knowing how to say no and ask for what you need

- The ability to express emotions

- The tendency to look at life positively

- The ability to move on quickly from bad experiences

- Having a healthy, realistic, and positive outlook on one's abilities

- Acceptance of one's own strengths and weaknesses

- The ability to accept both positive and negative feedback

It is easy to see how important healthy levels of self-esteem are in life, but good performance in work or school is not the cause of self-esteem. Self-esteem can be gained from good performance. It is more a determinant for risk one will take to further themselves in life.

As we noted earlier, there is a fine line between having high self-esteem and being overconfident even to the point of narcissism. People with excessive levels of self-esteem may see their lives as only successes, but a closer look at their life often paints a different picture. Overconfidence can easily alienate someone from those around them, and it can be a turn off in intimate relationships. Overconfident people are more likely to experience unnecessary conflict in life.

People with healthy levels of self-esteem make better leaders as they aren't afraid to speak up or be critical, but this skill can also lead to conflict. Not all conflict is a bad thing. Sometimes real problems can be solved with healthy conflict.

People with high levels of self-esteem report high levels of happiness and life satisfaction, whereas people with low self-esteem often report higher levels of anxiety and depression.

Those with high levels of self-esteem are more likely to take the initiative. They are more likely to experiment in life and this can be both good and bad depending on what that experimentation entails.

Self-esteem does not correlate with ability and talent. There are people with very high levels of self-esteem with little to no skill and highly talented people who think poorly of themselves. So inherent talent is not affected by self-esteem, but the success or risk we take with that talent may be.

With just this brief introduction, it is easy to see why self-esteem has long been a big concern and area of interest for people in the social sciences. It can have a profound impact on one's life and what they get from it. There is a debate in the social sciences about the value placed on self-esteem. There are those who think we overvalue it, and others feel like it needs to be the prime focus of research.

America has long been a country that fosters high levels of self-esteem, and data has shown these efforts have been effective. Americans tend to have higher levels of self-esteem than citizens of other countries, but there are a lot of debates about the usefulness of this data. Some say that the wording of the survey questions is leading and may inflate the subsequent data, leading to results that stray from actual reality.

Serious methodological issues make the study of self-esteem difficult and often ambiguous. Most often, self-esteem is measured through self-reporting, which is notoriously unreliable. The way a survey question is worded can also lead, which can affect the responses, and thus, the outcome of the study.

With self-reporting, there are tons of issues. People like to please – and often want to respond to how they feel presents themselves in the best light or that provide the answer the researcher wants to hear. People may answer untruthfully to feel better or to appear more socially acceptable, even if this isn't their inner reality.

This has led to developing more subtle measures harder for respondents to "fake." Measures like the Rosenberg Scale have grown in popularity, as it is a more reliable measure that is less prone to false reporting.

One of the biggest issues with testing for self-esteem is the need for objective measures that aren't affected by cultural and other factors, which is a lot harder than it might seem. This means we are likely to continue to struggle to find universally applicable measures of self-esteem. There is no area of the brain we can scan to get a reliable and unbiased number about the amount of self-esteem a person possesses.

This might lead some to think, "what's the point in studying something so slippery?" and the short answer is because it plays such a huge role in the outcome of people's lives. Self-esteem can affect how well one takes care of their physical and mental needs. It can affect what they choose to pursue or not.

We should close this brief introduction by noting that for many people, self-esteem can be variable depending on the circumstances they are facing in life. There are people who just seem to, innately, have high levels of self-esteem and those whose self-esteem is related to how much they fail or succeed in a given effort. Self-esteem is a much more complicated issue than many originally thought, and that means that high self-esteem is good and low self-esteem is bad is not inherently true.

Chapter 2: Understanding Self-Awareness

The concept of self-awareness also seems obvious at face value. Most would say they are self-aware, but when we look at this idea a little more closely, again, things start to change.

But much of what we do daily is done on autopilot. We have a set routine we are so used to following. Because of this, we do things with little conscious thought given to what we are doing and why. Most of us are unaware of how much of our life is spent this way.

We can think of self-awareness in terms of levels. First, "what am I doing?" Next, "what am I feeling?" And finally, "where are my blind spots?"

Life is obviously better than the alternative, but it isn't always great. We have to deal with failures, irritations, obligations, frustrations, and pain, but the flip side encases positive emotions of love, joy, success, and happiness. The tendency to avoid thinking about or confronting negative emotions is a natural human defense mechanism, but for many of us, this becomes our go-to response for any emotionally stressful or demanding situation. Often, we turn to defense mechanisms as opposed to tackling our feelings head-on.

Introspection

Introspection is a lot like awareness, but it is directly tied to the self and not an external actor or force. It refers to how much and how often we look inward and examine our thoughts, feelings, values.

We are very familiar with observation, which is an external focus on the world, but many of us aren't very familiar with introspection. It plays a key role in our ability to know, understand, and accept ourselves, which is a huge part of developing healthy levels of self-esteem. We rarely spend much time thinking about our mood states in the past and the present, why we feel this way, and what this might tell us about our situation and ourselves. This is something that interests philosophers and psychologists, but we would all do well to have a better understanding of what this means and how to use it.

When we think about learning, particularly about self, we might think of brain wave machine readouts or New Age-type things such as contacting our past lives, but that is missing the point and looking at the extremes.

Not all learning is book learning. Sometimes we have to harness our inner philosopher and just think about thinking. Think about feeling. Think about the source or root of our ideas, values. I can almost see eyes rolling right now as many of us feel like we are way too busy to participate in something like this, but we aren't, and we really should.

While we won't get in the weeds, there is a camp of philosophers that think that self-knowledge is the basis for acquiring any other knowledge, and if we want to have a better understanding of the world around us, it can be helpful to start with ourselves.

In today's world, so many of us are busy, and even when we aren't, we feel it's selfish to spend time on ourselves or think about our thoughts and feelings. We take away from work, from family, from our friends, and from whatever else. While too much introspection makes someone self-absorbed, the opposite isn't good either.

We have to make time for ourselves, mentally; otherwise, we will never understand the root of our behavior, what we are feeling, or why we are feeling that. If we want to take control of our lives and improve self-confidence, we will have to be willing to take a close, deep look within ourselves, no matter how difficult or uncomfortable it might make us.

Introspection might best be understood as a tool that can help develop self-awareness, which we will look at below. Not only is it a tool, but it is also a powerful one that can offer us with a great means to get to know ourselves as we are. But what, exactly, counts?

Well, making a sad face in the mirror and then assuming the emotion you are feeling is sadness is not how to do it. There is a lot of disagreement about what is specifically entailed as a part of the functional process of introspection, but it has to be a process that allows us to develop ideas about ourselves that we can test against different conditions such as thought experiments.

Introspection can only give us insight into our own minds, and nothing we learn from this can be generalized to anyone else. When we introspect, we are thinking about how we are feeling right now and probing more deeply into our thoughts to see what we can learn about ourselves from them.

It requires us to detect or directly acknowledge the mental state we are now in, to give us the basis from which we can analyze it.

Now, let's move on to self-awareness and the psychological theory surrounding it.

Self-Awareness Theory

Self-awareness is more complicated than it might first seem because it refers to more than just knowing and understanding yourself. It also refers to how realistically and accurately you view yourself. This might seem easy to do, but in practice, it proves otherwise.

It is likely impossible for us to find an accurate measure of our self-awareness, and it seems far-fetched that psychology will show us a way to quantify this shortly. But this doesn't mean we can't approximate it through introspection and understanding, which is something everyone should do.

Basically, self-awareness is more akin to degrees than any concrete amount of self-knowledge, but if we never look within and give our thoughts and the credence of our thoughts, we will have a hard time even reaching a healthy self-awareness level.

In 1972, Duval and Wicklund developed *the self-awareness theory.* The basic idea is that, at least in some way, who we are as a self is distinct from what we think and feel. As they said back in the 70s, "we are not our thoughts."

Most of us rarely, if ever, give our inner self much thought. We do so many things on autopilot, and much of our life consists of distractions, which we will look at below in greater detail.

It's not that we can't focus on our inner self; it's that most of us choose not to and live by a routine mindlessly where we rarely never give ourselves any regard. The ability for self-evaluation may be something unique to humankind, but it is a skill we should make more use of, considering it is so helpful in our journey towards healthy self-esteem.

When we do engage in self-evaluation, we often look at our thoughts and actions and measure how closely these come to our stated values and beliefs. This can be uncomfortable as there are times we may not like what we see, but that doesn't mean we need not see it. The more we learn about ourselves, the more we can change our mindset and control our behaviors in ways more in line with our values and beliefs.

In this theory, there are two possible outcomes of our self-evaluation. We either pass or fail. If we pass, it means we have determined that our thoughts and actions are in line with our beliefs and values. If we fail, it means we do not.

But here is where we need to step back. Where do our beliefs and values come from? This question is not as easy to answer as we might think. We pick up many of our beliefs and values from our family, our community, and society. Our values are often culturally based, which means they can vary across cultures.

With beliefs, these, too, are largely derived from our family, where we live, our education.

But what we are likely to find when we practice introspection is that many of our values and beliefs are a lot hollower than we might have thought. Do we even understand why we hold the values we do? What is the evidential basis for our beliefs? Are they even corroborated with evidence, and if so, how does one deal with the cognitive dissonance of discovering one holds *false* beliefs?

We can't provide the answers to these deep questions in a short book, but this little window should go to show just how shaky our internal life often is when we don't give it much thought and regard. Our brain takes mental shortcuts that allow us to continue our autopilot routine, which can cause us to develop what we think are ingrained beliefs not supported by reality.

Our idea of what passing and failing will look like and what standards have to be met will also vary from person to person. So, this is not a very objective measure; but then, it is hard to see how it can be. While it might not stand up to scientific rigor, it does give us a decent understanding of where we think our life is versus where we think it *should be.*

When we find ourselves failing at living by our values and standards, there are only two options. We can adjust our standards so we now meet them, or we can work to change our actions and behavior, so it comes more in line with the things we think, feel, and believe. The other option is to choose distraction and simply not think about it.

If this is what you were going to do, you probably wouldn't be reading this book! So, let's continue on.

We do have control over the standards we place on ourselves, and it isn't necessarily a bad thing to revisit and rethink them. Many of us hold ourselves to a much higher standard than we would anyone else, and obviously, this isn't fair.

We might also have unrealistic expectations for ourselves that, when we invariably fail to meet them, make us feel like we are failures in life that can't live up to our perceived potential. As much as we would like to think we could all be rock stars and football players, we must be honest with ourselves, not kick ourselves and let that negative inner critic take over. Because you, as someone with poor eyesight, could never be an airplane pilot, for instance. That just isn't a reasonable expectation for us to hold for ourselves.

In our evaluation, we might also find we are placing way too much emphasis on a successful outcome and not enough on our *performance.* The amount of effort we put into something is a thing we need to pat ourselves on the back for, regardless of how it turned out. A good performance is a good performance, regardless of the results. A lesson we will see repeatedly in this book is that we must cut ourselves some slack.

Developing a good sense of self-awareness helps us to become more proactive and is likely to boost the confidence we have in our thoughts and abilities because we have consciously considered them, rather than simply making assumptions about ourselves.

The more aware we are of ourselves, the more in control of our actions and feelings we become. While we won't be able to stop from feeling a certain way, with time and effort, we can understand why we react a certain way to a given situation. If this reaction is negative, ways we can exhibit more self-control, so these feelings don't cause issues in our life.

Psychologists Ridley, Schultz, Glanz, and Weinstein found in 1992 research that people with a good degree of self-awareness also tend to make better decisions for themselves and their lives. This shouldn't be too surprising as the more we know and understand about something, the better our assumptions and ideas about it will be, even when that something is ourselves.

Distraction

For many of us, distraction is our response to bad news and negative emotions. It allows us to move on without having to face the issue that may prove uncomfortable or difficult, but distraction is also a good thing. It is a healthy reaction since it wouldn't be good for our physical or mental well-being if we could never let go of life's problems and lose ourselves in something mundane.

Distraction is a healthy defense mechanism that allows us to deal with unavoidable stresses, but the problem arises when distraction is our only response to stress or negative issues. Our refusal to face a negative reality can cause more problems than it is worth.

Not that one should avoid distraction; as we noted above, it is a useful and healthy way of dealing with reality. It can be vital for our mental and physical health. The key is to be aware of distractions and when we use them. Distraction can also become autopilot, like so many other parts of life.

Are you in control of your distractions, or are you simply on autopilot? The goal is to be more in control of our use of distractions so we can be more discerning about when to employ them. We should consciously choose distractions rather than mindlessly engage in it. You must pay attention to yourself, and what you are doing so you know when you are "checking out" of reality and how long you did this.

Distraction is everywhere, from scrolling through social media to daydreaming. We often do this with little awareness of the fact that we are doing this. Do you know how you are using your time? When we pay attention to what we do, we often find that a lot more of our life is spent on distractions we had originally assumed. As we pay more attention to our actions and what we are doing with our time, we can take more control of our life.

This is also important with interpersonal relationships. We often think we are more present and better listeners than we are. This can have an impact on the quality of our relationships. Sometimes our distractions are causing us to disconnect or alienate those around us, and we may not even know this is happening.

Again, it is important to say that we don't recommend eliminating distractions. They are fun and often a useful part of our lives that gives it meaning and value. We just need to become cognizant of when we are employing distraction, how long we are doing it, and can pull ourselves out when we realize we are using it at the wrong time.

It is easy to distract ourselves to where it becomes routine - we want to avoid this and correct that tendency. When you notice you've checked out, don't simply snap back to reality. Consider the surrounding situation. Do you do this at work? Around family and friends? Consider what it is about these situations causes you to reach for distraction.

We must be able to look at these situations objectively and without judgment. Otherwise, we cannot address what is causing us to turn to distraction rather than be present in that moment. For example, say I wear headphones everywhere I go. If I think about it on the surface, I might just think I enjoy listening to music. While this is certainly true, what is the reason I reach for my earbuds any time I'm in public? For me, it is a defense mechanism against social interaction – a fear of people.

What Are We Feeling?

So we can see how we use distraction, almost without notice, to avoid being present and aware of our lives and what is going on in and around them, but it isn't enough to just know what you are doing; it is also important to understand what you are feeling.

We often feel emotions, even intense ones, but don't know how to find or pinpoint what exactly it is we are feeling and why. It's hard to pinpoint the source of emotions if you don't even know what it is you are feeling at a given moment.

Reducing and controlling distractions, as we talked about in the previous section, means we will be more present in our lives and thus must deal with emotions. This can be uncomfortable and confusing, especially at first. Many people avoid and don't like thinking about their emotions because it just feels so big and overwhelming. The more intensely we feel them, the less we want to face them, it seems.

When you come face-to-face with your emotions, you discover your true self and how you feel about things in life. Learning about self will be inherently uncomfortable, largely, because it is something we seem to disregard.

As we talked about above, learning and controlling distraction isn't nearly as personal or emotionally rife as figuring out what and why we are feeling this way. Often, people have a much easier time with that than developing self-awareness.

It is likely to take a long time to understand what you are feeling and the possible sources of a emotion. Many people spend years in therapy trying to figure out their emotions and the source of feelings so deeply felt. Also, to make things more difficult, emotions are ever present and often have no profound meaning or source. Sometimes we are happy because we saw something cute and for no other more profound reason than that. Over time and with reflection, you can separate feelings that need to be probed and addressed from random feelings that are simply the result of being human.

Here's where things get even more confusing. Human emotions can, in themselves, be distractions. For example, I might mire myself in an endless stream of cute kitten videos so I can feel happy even when my life is falling apart around me. I am using the kittens as a happiness distraction, so I need not address real issues in my life.

Examining emotions will, naturally, lead to other emotions, causing us to delve into an endless spiral of self-reflection. We always want to peel back one more layer of the proverbial onion to see what's underneath, but there comes a point where it becomes counterproductive to our efforts.

Experts recommend going just a few layers down into our emotions and being content with what we learn. Otherwise, we will end up in an unhealthy loop of self-inquiry.

We must also address our blind spots if we wish to become more self-aware. All this self-reflection may make you realize how empty and hollow many of our thoughts and opinions are. So much of our life is spent reacting to how we feel at a moment rather than acting consciously and with forethought. We aren't as deliberate or rational as we would like to think, and emotion directs our behavior a lot more than we realize.

The mind is a finicky thing and has a lot of blind spots that are helpful to understand. Memory is inherently unreliable. We overestimate how much we really know about a subject and often even our abilities. We don't always change our minds in the face of conflicting evidence; some of us may even double down. We focus on things that mesh with our view of reality and ignore those that might make us rethink our beliefs.

While these may seem like (and can be) serious issues we can do little about, being aware of them is part and parcel of self-awareness. It is understanding the inherent issues all humans deal with. We must accept them during this process of self-discovery, becoming more self-aware that our beliefs and values are often weaker and less backed by evidence than we may have thought.

We need to learn our patterns of behavior and action so we can put the brakes on negative responses or inappropriate uses of distraction. We also must be realistic about how much we can do to counter the natural pitfalls we all deal with. Being aware of it won't stop them but it is useful in helping us understand others and ourselves.

Developing Self-Awareness and How We Sabotage Ourselves

While a lot of self-awareness is accepting things about ourselves that we cannot change, there are a lot of ways we can foster self-awareness. Mindfulness, or being present and closely observing one's emotional and physical state, is an useful way to gain more self-awareness. Mediation can also be helpful and can be used with other mindfulness strategies. We will discuss meditation in more detail in a later chapter.

Keeping a journal or diary is also a great way to foster self-awareness. Putting something into words requires us to look more closely at our emotions. Talking to others is also useful, and accepting the feedback they can give you - whether it is positive or negative. These things are done in pursuing self-awareness and the greater goal of self-acceptance.

We can do many things to improve the way we see the world and our responses to it that will help foster greater self-esteem, more happiness, and a sense of purpose in our lives. Then, by doing these things, we also become more empathetic with others, and ourselves, which is also a huge benefit.

Seeing ourselves more clearly allows us to better gauge our skill and ability, which can make it easier to decide when it makes sense to take the risk. It can lead to more confidence and an outpouring of creativity. Self-awareness can also help us improve our communication with others, which can enhance interpersonal relationships.

We can just as easily sabotage our efforts as we can benefit from new knowledge and understanding. Self-doubt is a huge killer. It will keep us from even trying due to fear of failure. To a certain extent, doubt is a good thing, as it makes us seek outside opinions, question ourselves, and become more accepting of the change. But excessive levels of doubt cripple us and keep up from taking risks and trying new things.

We shouldn't fear doubt, as it can be helpful, but we need to learn how to control and harness it, so it doesn't run our lives. Having excessive doubt will make us less likely to express our emotions and needs, as we are unsure of ourselves. It can even cause us to lose control over our lives, letting others guide our lives and make our decisions for us.

Chapter 3: Calculating Your Self-Worth

Our feelings of self-worth are often closely tied to self-esteem, which makes perfect sense. Self-worth refers to how we feel about our inherent value, how we stack up against others, and how deserving we are of success and/or happiness. For those with low self-esteem, our sense of self-worth is also often lacking.

People with low self-worth often think that others are more deserving of happiness and success than they are. This can become a self-fulfilling prophecy because if we feel this way we are less likely to take risks or initiatives that could lead us closer to our goals in life.

For all our concern about self-love and valuing the inherent worth of human life, there often isn't a lot of actionable advice on how to foster a sense of self-worth. There are quite a few things that have proven to be highly successful at fostering self-worth, such as daily mantras (we will talk about this in a later chapter) or concern and well wishes from others. But how can we internalize feelings of self-worth so we believe in our worth and value?

Here, we want to look at how to better manage life and its stresses and to develop a better understanding of ourselves that allows us to grow and progress. While their heart may be in the right place, the "you're doing great, sweetie" and "it will all be okay" platitudes don't provide any actual help.

What is Self-Worth? And Why is it Important?

The short definition of self-worth simply refers to the value you place on yourself, especially compared with the value you place on other people. It is an important part of self-esteem, and while it might not be clear at first, having unhealthy feelings about your own self-worth can have a hugely detrimental effect on your life and wellbeing.

People who don't feel like they have value are often unsure of themselves, their thoughts, and their opinions. They aren't likely to speak up when someone says something they don't agree with or something that hurts their feelings.

So, we are less likely to stand up for ourselves when we have low self-worth, and we are also less likely to take risks and make changes that might make our lives better, such as obtaining an education or even getting out of a bad relationship.

Just as important, people who lack self-worth are not nearly as likely to engage in self-care. This means they ignore their physical, mental, and emotional needs, which, in turn, may lead to even worse self-confidence and more.

While it might not be obvious at first, our emotional state can be directly related to the value we place on ourselves. The way we handle stress. How we approach emotionally charged situations and more. Perhaps now it is becoming clearer just how negative feelings of self-worth can dramatically affect our daily lives, our overall health and our wellbeing.

There are psychological theories about self-worth that relate one's feelings of personal value through competition with others. In this theory, the value we place on ourselves is directly related to how we think we stack up against other people.

In today's world of celebrity culture and social media, this can have a profoundly negative impact on our feelings of self-worth. We will touch on this in greater detail below, but suffice to say that we most often engage in *upward comparison*. We compare ourselves with the most successful, beautiful, etc., .and thus, are not nearly as likely to feel we stack up like if we compared ourselves with our peers or even ourselves, for instance.

People commonly measure their self-worth based on the upward comparison, but we also measure it based on how we feel we stack up against people we know. Some of us also place value based on the type of people we know. How many important people are in your social circle? For some, this might have a huge impact on how we feel about ourselves.

The way we look and feel is another key factor we use to determine our own self-worth. If we feel like everyone else is more attractive and more stable than us, we are less likely to feel as if we have as much value as those around us.

Our occupation or what we do for a living can also affect how we feel we stack up against others. If we feel like we have an important or "good" job, we are likely to feel more worthy than how someone in a "dead-end job" feels about himself or herself. We will discuss the pitfalls of place personal value on career accomplishments later.

We might also measure our value based on our material success and the stuff we have. If we have a nice house with tons of toys and gadgets, we may feel more worthy and valuable than someone living in a trailer park, struggling from paycheck to paycheck. We will talk about how these factors should do not pertain to how we feel about our worth to society, but the fact is that many of us use this as our guidepost.

How Did We Get Here and Where Do We Go?

Far too many of us are "broken" or "damaged" from negative or traumatic life experiences. Perhaps we have seen a lot of loss in our lives, had unstable family situations or were mistreated or neglected. With all this in mind, it is easy to see why so many of us have a hard time calculating our value and improving our sense of self-worth.

There are several definitions of self-worth, but many relate to life success and how well you have kept to the goals you set for yourself. This might not be the best measure of self-worth since there are plenty of people with a great amount of skill, talent, and work ethic who struggle in life for reasons outside of their control. The main problem with this idea of self-worth is that accomplishments don't make someone more valuable than anyone else - all humans are valuable, and this should be nurtured and fostered in all of us, regardless of our material success.

Self-worth and self-love don't mean just constantly telling yourself that you are great. This might be part of it, but the real goal is to take care of you - physically, mentally, and spiritually. It means learning about and accepting your strengths, weaknesses, and quirks. It is learning to accept that you aren't perfect and that it's okay - nobody is perfect.

There are many reasons it can be difficult for someone to acknowledge their self-worth. Some of us grow up in unhealthy environments that lack love and positive feedback. Others grew up in the shadow of someone they could never hope to "keep up with" in terms of achievement. Perhaps you had parents with a bad relationship, who treated each other poorly, and this was your only source of knowledge and guidance.

Any – or all – of these things can contribute to negative feelings of self-worth. It can make it hard for us to see and accept our own value as humans, but we will say it again, and again, it is there. All humans are inherently worthy and valuable. A lack of self-worth can affect one's daily life.

It can make it more difficult for us to have happy and successful interpersonal relationships and careers. If we don't see our value, we are more likely to accept mistreatment or mediocrity in life. These things can then reduce our feelings of self-worth even more and become yet another vicious cycle.

There is no step-by-step process for developing better feelings of self-worth. It is hard and can be a long process, but the main thing we will need to do is that adage from the Oracle at Delphi: know thyself. We need to learn how to have self-compassion, accept responsibility for our lives, accept our weaknesses besides our strengths, and know that the biggest impediment to our happiness is often us.

People in your life may be contributing to your lack of feeling of self-worth. Perhaps someone constantly criticizes you and has nothing nice to say. This is not helpful to the journey we are trying to take, and it might be a good idea to reduce the influence this person has over your life or cut them out entirely.

You need to take care of yourself, physically and mentally. Evaluating how you use your time, such as how you use and react to social media, can also really help us have a more positive sense of self-worth. We will discuss social media and celebrity culture and how this relates to our self-esteem in a later chapter.

The Tricky Nature of Self-Worth

Like our self-esteem, our feeling of self-worth can be variable with time and circumstance. Our self-worth isn't something many of us think about often or deeply. Sure, we might feel like we have value, but then we reach a stumbling block or experience failure. Then, our feelings of worth and value take a big hit. We rarely see how much of an impact this can have on our lives.

Many people measure their self-worth based on how they stack up against others. This might be in terms of looks, money, career success. These things can affect how we think about ourselves and how we feel like we stack up in society. Though these things have their importance, all people have inherent worth and value, even if they "contribute little" in the classical sense to society.

The measuring stick should be yourself, not your social betters. Look at where you've come from, know who you are, and it will help you come to terms with and accept whom you are. This doesn't mean you shouldn't try to change or improve the things in your life you have control over. Although, it does mean there are elements of your personality that are constant, regardless of outside factors and life experience. These are the things we need to accept as they are.

Learning to cultivate your sense of self-worth will help you come to believe that, as a human, you are enough and deserve love and respect.

In psychology, the self-worth theory posits that our main goal in life is the search for self-acceptance. Many achieve this through material and career success, through competition with others, and through relationships and personal connections. Too many, we calculate our self-worth through constant effort and competition.

The main elements of this theory include ability, effort, performance, and self-worth. It is easy to see how the first three elements might have a determining effect on the fourth. Your abilities (or how you perceive them) are likely to affect your level of effort, which will affect your performance, leading to a self-perpetuating cycle.

The main problem with this theory is that the emphasis is placed on accomplishment, which need not be tied to self-worth. Though this shouldn't be the case, most of us evaluate our self-worth based on effort and accomplishment and how we compare to others.

But achieving goals is great, but your ability or inability to achieve these goals does not reduce your worth. Having a prestigious job isn't a measure of worth; the important part is that you are fulfilled by what you do. A social media following does not define worth, nor do the relationships you do or don't have. Getting older doesn't make you less worthy or valuable, either, despite the value we place on youth in our society.

It is easier to fix your sense of self-worth as a younger person, but that choice has long passed for most of us. First, we must look at things that contribute to our self-worth and learn to internalize this. Identify your inner critic quick to negativity and constantly focuses on failure. It's important to be able to criticize ourselves so we make better decisions, but too often, that negative inner critic is the driving force of how we feel about ourselves, and *that voice isn't always right.*

When you notice that inner critic coming to the fore, step back and think about what that critic is saying. Is it correct? Does it help you to become better? If it is and will, listen to it. If not, ignore it or argue with it. Challenge the voice when it is unnecessarily critical.

To form and maintain mutually beneficial relationships, we need to a positive sense of self-worth lest we end up with someone who dominates or constantly criticizes us and ultimately makes us feel even worse about ourselves. We must be able to communicate effectively. Being loved is not what makes us worthy of love; we are worthy of that inherently. Our intimate relationships should be partnerships; they are not our saviors.

Loving and accepting ourselves makes it easier to love and accept others. It will help us have better interpersonal relationships with family, friends, coworkers, etc.

Self-worth should never be tied to something outside of you. You still have value and worth even if you lose your job or fail to obtain that promotion. Jobs can be transient, and to base our entire sense of self and personal value on something transient is dangerous.

Many psychologists use something called the self-worth scale to allow people to see how they value themselves. Called the Contingencies of Self-Worth, this scale was developed by Crocker, Luhtanen, Cooper, and Bourvrette in 2003. The scale consists of 35 items that evaluate self-worth based on seven "domains."

The Seven Domains

- Approval from others (do we care about what others think about us?)

- Physical appearance (how do we feel like we stack up looks wise?)

- Outdoing others in the competition (how much do we derive worth from doing better than our peers?)

- Academic competence (do we base our self-worth on academic achievement?)

- Family and support (do we need support from family and friends to feel worthy?)

- Being virtuous and moral (do we derive our worth from our acts?)

- God's love (do we have only value if God loves us?)

The scale is rated from 1 (strongly disagree) to 7 (strongly agree). The total number is summed and divided by 5 to get a subscale score. This scale has shown to be accurate and useful to people studying self-worth.

There are many exercises online, including interactive lessons and worksheets, that you can use to help you determine your current feelings of self-worth and to improve them by building up your confidence. These can be very helpful for people who need guidance or are unsure of where to start.

More research needs to be done, just like all other self-esteem research areas, but what we know shows how important it is for our very quality of life to have a healthy level of feelings of self-worth.

Chapter 4: Learning Self-Acceptance

Acceptance is one of those things that seem simple on their surface but prove difficult in action. Most of us have a much easier time accepting and forgiving others than we do ourselves. We tend to be much harder on ourselves than we are on those around us. You don't achieve self-acceptance, and then - boom - you're done, and you have it for life. Rather, it is something that you will probably have to work hard on and perhaps even in perpetuity.

For some, a small setback can make it difficult to look inwardly with love and compassion. All we see is that we made mistakes, we don't look at the struggles we faced or what we overcame; all we see is the result. But life will include failure, it will happen, and that's okay. It doesn't mean we are lesser people who don't deserve love or respect.

So, while many struggle with it, self-acceptance is something we can cultivate with effort, and we will be better and happier people for our effort, even when it's hard.

What Is Self-Acceptance?

Self-acceptance is one term that seems self-evident; however, it may not be as clear as it initially seems. We all want to accept and love ourselves for who we are, which is easier said than done. But with acceptance, what about the parts we don't like or those we wish we could change about ourselves?

The inability to accept negative things or weaknesses about us that are outside of our control to change is a huge impediment to self-acceptance. It is one thing to accept the good things about ourselves, our strengths and attributes, that we feel make us valuable to society, but self-acceptance isn't just about the things we are proud of.

We are humans. All humans are imperfect, and even the person with the highest amount of self-esteem is likely to have a thing or two about themselves that they wish they could change but cannot. The real struggle here is to accept those things too.

There is a lot about who we are that we have control over and can change. On the flip side, there are parts of our personality incredibly difficult or impossible to change. For example, say I am super sensitive. There really isn't much I can do about this, as the feelings and emotions come whether I want them to or not. I may not like this part of myself, but I might not have the ability to change this. Self-acceptance doesn't mean liking these things about yourself, but accepting that they are what they are.

For things like meditation and mindfulness practice, which we look at in more detail below, to have a positive impact, we need to accept ourselves for who and what we are.

It might sound strange, but there is also evidence that lacking self-acceptance can make your experience of certain illnesses or health conditions worse.

It appears there are even differences in the structure of the brain of people who lack self-acceptance. The part of the brain that controls emotions and stress has less gray matter in people with low-self acceptance than those with high self-acceptance. There may also be a lack of gray matter in the areas responsible for controlling stress and anxiety.

An impediment like this might seem all but impossible to overcome, but we can change this. The brain is a complicated and sophisticated organ, and the "paths" we wear in our brain become ingrained, so that is the path our neurons are most likely to follow, but this doesn't mean we cannot create new paths. It takes time and conscious effort, but it is possible.

How Do We Cultivate Self-Acceptance?

We must go into self-acceptance with an open heart and mind. This may require us to change our way of thinking about our circumstances and ourselves and to leave blame behind. We must let go of our feelings of shame and doubt and to open ourselves to positive feelings that move beyond the things that hold us back.

We must move beyond self-hatred and inner criticism. These things do nothing other than holding us back and dislike ourselves for things beyond our control or that we cannot change.

We need to celebrate our strengths, and yes, we all have them, even if they seem useless or inconsequential. Say you are a good knitter. This might seem like it isn't that important, but it is considered a strength that not everyone can do. Count it as a strength that is just as important as career success. Ask yourself questions: Am I kind? Am I good at activity "x"? Do I have a real skill for a hobby? These things are invaluable strengths you should note and be proud of. Think about obstacles or hardships you have overcome. These, too, are strengths.

You will need to consider your social circle. What type of people do you have in your social circle, and why are they a part of your life? Part of self-acceptance might also mean accepting there can be people that are toxic and keep you from being your best self. Consider letting them go or reducing their influence on your life.

Create your support network because we do get to choose our friends. We might not have control over who makes up our family, but we control how much influence we let them have on our lives. We have a lot more control with our friends. Our social circle should be compromised of people who have mutually beneficial relationships. We should uplift our friends, and they should uplift us; real friendship isn't a competition.

Just like you should love and respect your friends, you should have the expectation they will love and respect you.

Self-acceptance will require you to forgive yourself. We have all done things we aren't proud of or regret. We can learn from these mistakes and try to live a better life, and that is how we should take these things. For too many of us, we never forgive ourselves or let go of these failures. We carry around shame and regret over things we cannot change, which hinders our forward progress.

You must be able to forgive yourself and realize that you are not the sum of your mistakes. We learn and grow from our errors and then move on.

Another part of self-acceptance that is related to forgiving ourselves is learning how to shut our inner critic up when it isn't helpful.

It is also okay to mourn our dreams and things unrealized. There is no shame in being upset or regretful about the road you didn't travel. When we were kids, we had such idealized dreams of our future, and most of us don't get there. This is life, but it is okay to be sad about what could have been, but don't get mired in it.

Allow yourself to feel sad but then move on, don't get mired in what could have, would have, or should have been.

No matter what your station in life, you can do good deeds, whether it is to donate money or volunteer your time. Helping others allows us to use our time and resources for the greater good. Not only will this make you feel good and do something great for society, but it will also make it easier to argue with that inner critic about your value. It is hard to argue that you are a bad person with no value if you spend your time working for the good of other people.

Acceptance Isn't Resignation

Accepting yourself for who you are, including the mistakes you may have made in the past, is not resignation. This doesn't mean you are burying the notion that you can change or become a better person. Rather, it is simply acknowledging where and who you are at this point in your life.

Whether acceptance stops at this awareness or motivates them to move forward towards a greater goal is up to the individual.

It makes sense to focus our energy on things we have control over. Say you have "two left feet." This means you will never be a star athlete, but that doesn't mean you can't pursue the sport you love with friends or as part of a community effort. It is an effort of rethinking our goals based on our current status and actual abilities.

When trying to learn to love and accept yourself, try to speak to the best you—the self-actualized, best possible version of yourself. Consider what you might do or say in a given situation and give it a listen or even a try.

None of us will ever be completely happy with our lives or ourselves. We are all human, and we need to be accepting and mindful of this. Work hard to stop cutting yourself down or undercutting your potential. You need to be realistic about what it is possible to achieve and make goals based on your actual abilities.

Being kind to yourself is not selfish; it is a basic part of self-care that too many of us neglect. It is vital to living a happy and fulfilled life. While we may not see it, failure and setbacks are part of being humans, and even the most successful person in life experiences this. Love you, flaws and all, and work to change elements of your personality and life you have control over. So, for example, you can't help being upset by something, but you can help how you react or respond to it.

If asked, most of us would say we are okay with who we are and what we have become, but deeper probing shows how untrue this is. Most of us have issues in our own life, unlikeable things about ourselves or regrets we haven't accepted. This is natural, and the problem lies not with the fact that we have regrets or things about ourselves that we don't like, but our refusal to accept these things.

This probing, while uncomfortable, is important to self-knowledge and, ultimately, self-acceptance. Carl Rogers, one of the first psychologists to discuss the importance of positive self-regard, focused on the importance of positive self-regard on our overall mental health and happiness. We must be open to others and can think positively about ourselves. This, Rogers thought, helped us function in the world and in turn, helped us get over negative thoughts and experiences more quickly. He believed that negativity acts as a destructive force that will cause negative issues in life if unaddressed.

Chapter 5: Taking Self-Responsibility

When most of us think of the word "responsibility," we think of the obligations we have in our lives, such as our careers or our children, but it has a slightly different meaning in the psychological community we will need to unpack.

Think about the question, "do you own your life?" Most of us would immediately respond, "yes, of course," but how true is that, really? Just like with self-acceptance, it isn't always true that we own our lives upon closer inspection. For many of us, we are owned by our jobs or the roles we play in society. While this is common, it can also stand in the way of living a happy and meaningful life.

Responsibility naturally makes us think about the obligations or consequences of our actions, which is part of what the word means, but with relation to ourselves, it is a bit more nuanced. Basically, it is a form of acceptance that allows us to take more control over our own lives (or let other entities take control).

Basically, self-responsibility refers to understanding that our thoughts, emotions, and behaviors are our own and impact our life experience. Yes there are outside factors at play, but this remains true on the day-to-day level.

To have healthy self-esteem and live your best life, understand that you, your thoughts, and your actions are responsible for much of your external experience.

How often do we blame others or outside circumstances for the state of our lives? It is far easier to do this than to look inward to see where you contributed and to make changes.

What, Exactly, is Self-Responsibility?

In psychology, *self-responsibility* is also often called *personal responsibility*. This refers to the amount of accountability we feel or place on ourselves for our actions and feelings. This might seem like a fairly new concept, but it has ancient roots, though what it means to be personally responsible, of course, changes with time and place.

The concept of self-responsibility works on the assumption that as individuals, we have some degree of personal autonomy that allows us to decide and act in our lives in response to circumstances or stimuli surrounding us. This is, inherently, not a deterministic viewpoint. It holds we have free will, and along with that comes the responsibility and accountability for the things we say and do.

And this concept presupposes that we have at least control of our responses to our emotions and how we look at society. We can think, judge, decide, and act, and for these things, many believe that we need to take responsibility for.

While there is no way to control the emotions, we feel in response to stimuli or outside circumstances, this theory suggests that we can control our reaction and subsequent behavior and take ownership of these things.

Only in societies where the emphasis is placed solely on the individual is this possible. The individual or self has always been an important part of Western culture, so it shouldn't be surprising that self-responsibility concepts have taken root in the West.

When people have rights, they also have responsibility. As we have gained more human rights in the West, this, too, means we hold a lot more responsibility for how we treat others, our thoughts, our reactions, and ourselves. We are expected to be responsible citizens, responsible adults, responsible employees, parents, etc.

Since we have rights to resources and obligations to those around us, we are tasked with taking charge of how well (or not well) we take responsibility for these things.

Most of us probably think we take personal responsibility, but that isn't necessarily the case. How many of us look to outside forces, factors, or actors we can blame for our life's status, our reaction to something? It is so much easier to point to something outside of oneself than to look inward to see how your emotional state may have contributed to a situation.

Like a lot of what we must do to bolster our self-esteem, taking personal responsibility isn't fun, and it can even be difficult. Many of us settle into our role as the person pulled many ways by all these outside forces beyond our control, taking away our autonomy, and thus, our responsibility for our reactions and responses.

We must break this if we want to cultivate and internalize self-responsibility.

Are You Taking Self-Responsibility?

A good way to know if you are taking self-responsibility is to ask yourself if the thoughts, emotions, and behaviors you are exhibiting help or hinder you from reaching the goal you are trying to reach? We may not be able to control our emotions in terms of how something makes us feel, but we can control how we react and take responsibility for the fact that our actions are often a result of our own emotions, not some outside factor.

We are not only responsible for the way we react to our emotions, but also, we are responsible for how we use our time and how well we care for our mental, physical, and emotional needs.

Ways to Foster Self-Responsibility

Will Joel Friedman, Ph.D., offers a helpful list of ways you can learn to take self-responsibility in your life. The first and most important way to foster this is to be present at the moment. You must be aware of your surroundings, what you are doing, and how you are feeling to take full ownership over yourself.

You will need to be honest with yourself, perhaps brutally so. None of us like accepting that something is our fault, but part of growing and developing healthy levels of confidence and feelings of self-worth make this necessary. We can never grow, change, or adapt our responses if we refuse to admit that we make mistakes or have responsibility for negative situations in our life.

Friedman notes we are responsible for what come out of our mouth, and too often, we aren't careful enough in thinking about what we say before we say it. It isn't hard to see how this cannot only get us in trouble, but is our own fault.

We also need to be consistent in our thoughts and actions. We must accept that we don't know and will never know everything about the world – or even ourselves. The goal is to learn, accept, and take responsibility – not to become a self-guru of sorts.

He also points out that life should be win/win. What he means by this is that actions should be taken into consideration more than just you. We must think about our actions in terms of their effects on others and how it affects the greater good.

Finally, he discusses the importance of being willing to change and grow. Learning about ourselves is going to bring up uncomfortable feelings and show us areas of our personality we may not be proud of or like. While some things can't be changed and just must be accepted, a lot can be changed. To take self-responsibility, you must commit to being willing to grow and change as you learn more about yourself and others.

Focusing on the external environment as the cause of our life circumstances is a mental shortcut that keeps us from seeing the key role we play. Breaking down the barrier to this understanding is key to taking self-responsibility and working to make positive changes in your life.

Chapter 6: Practicing Self-Assertiveness

Before we even begin with this chapter, we have to say a word or two about assertiveness. We all know people who are overly assertive to the point of being demanding, and nobody suggests that this is something for which we should strive. There are many who lack the ability to stand up for themselves and ask for what they need, and when referring to assertiveness here, we are this referring to.

We are talking about people who lack self-confidence and find it hard to speak up with their opinions, express their needs and emotions, or challenge someone when necessary. It's that idea of being a doormat we discussed earlier. People without healthy levels of self-assertiveness let other people dominate conversations and their life, regardless of how they feel about it inside.

What we seek to do in this chapter is to discuss the difference between being healthily assertive and aggressive, and how being too nice leads us to live inauthentic lives and can negatively affect our relationships.

The Downside of Being Nice

Being nice is good, and for some people, it should be strived for more often, but it has its limitations, and there comes the point when it turns from a positive to a negative attribute. Lest you become that metaphorical doormat, you must put a limit on your kindness for yourself and others.

But being nice isn't always the same as being honest. To avoid potential conflict or discomfort, the overly nice person may just tell others what they think they want to hear, even if it isn't true, and they don't believe it. If we are striving for authenticity in life, it should be easy to see how this is a bad thing. Authenticity means honesty, even if it is uncomfortable to do.

What seemed like a positive trait can turn into a flaw if relied upon too often. What was once a noble characteristic becomes a wall you put between the real you and the people surrounding you. Many people who are overly nice feel (and are largely right) that they are not in control over their lives and are controlled by the surrounding people.

The goal is to understand that we are doing this, and we can take back control and put ourselves in charge.

Relationships aren't and can't be as fulfilling as they could be when one party is so nice they aren't showing their true self. This can make it hard for an overly nice person to develop deep interpersonal relationships. We need not stop being nice, but we do have to stop being nice all the time, and especially telling people what we think they want to hear rather than what we think.

Our relationships will be more fulfilling when we can be honest with both others and ourselves. When we can assert ourselves at the right level, we are truly partners in our relationships. Saying what you think and ask for what you need allows your partner to give that to you. It will help your relationships become deeper and more real.

What Does it Mean to Be Self-Assertive and Why Does It Matter?

We have touched on why being self-assertive matters, but first, we should step back and look at what it means to be assertive. Then, we can dive deeper on why it is so important to cultivate self-assertiveness; beyond the brief reasons we have given.

Chances are, if you lack assertiveness, you have been told before that you need to learn to stand up for yourself and be more vocal about your wants and needs. Like everything else we discuss in this book, that is a lot easier said than done.

What even is assertiveness? It refers to your confidence and ability to communicate your thoughts, needs, feelings, and beliefs openly and honestly. It is feeling unsure about our opinions and us. We want to assert ourselves without going to the point of violating others' rights or needs, which psychologists call *aggressiveness* and which we will touch on below.

There are a lot of misconceptions about assertiveness we should look at briefly. Being assertive does not mean getting what you want all the time. That isn't the point and shouldn't be the goal. Sometimes it will mean getting what you want, but more than anything, it is ensuring that your thoughts, feelings, and needs are addressed and those of other people and not instead of.

Being assertive isn't a universal trait we have to exhibit. Sometimes, call for being assertive and others where it isn't necessary. You are making a mistake if you assume that to self-assert, you must do so in every interpersonal interaction. Doing so will probably lead to conflict and unnecessary stress.

Failure to assert oneself can have a huge effect on self-esteem. It can make you feel as if your thoughts, feelings, and needs don't matter, and over time, you stop putting any emphasis on your own personal needs. People who cannot assert themselves often live lives directed and controlled (whether knowingly or not) by those around them.

People unable to express their thoughts or needs often keep them to themselves, even in situations it would benefit them to express their needs. This can lead to increased anxiousness, depression, and even resentment towards the people we have relinquished control to. Seeing as how it was us that relinquished control, it isn't fair to blame others for this situation.

People with generalized or social anxiety often report great difficulty asserting themselves in their daily lives. We fear ridicule and judgment, which can cause us to retract from society and develop unhealthy relationships with the people we interact with.

Assertiveness, or a lack thereof, is a learned skill. It is something we develop throughout our life experiences. Take a baby, for example. They cry when they want or need something and will learn to adapt their behavior to get most easily what they want or need. Adults do this, as well.

A baby (or a child or an adult) that doesn't get a positive response when they try to ask for what they need may develop a tendency to fail to assert to get what they need. If you come from a family where one member dominates the rest or unhealthy dialogue and communication is the norm, you may have self-assertiveness issues.

Some peer groups may even make you feel bad or selfish for having your own wants and needs, and we learn this over time, which leads us to shut off this part of ourselves. Due to this, we can turn into that figurative doormat easily.

A lot of things keep us from asserting ourselves when we need to. Many of us have a loud inner critic that tells us we lack, that we don't have the right skill or talent, and that we will embarrass ourselves if we express our opinions aloud. For many of us, this is enough to stifle us to the point we can't assert ourselves.

Some of us just don't have the skills or practice necessary to be self-assertive. The key is to learn and develop these skills so you can gain enough confidence to assert yourself inappropriate situations.

Being stressed or dealing with high anxiety can often shut us down, figuratively. It can make asserting ourselves feel like an impossible or pointless task. The problem is that failure to be assertive can also create higher levels of anxiety or stress. It can become a vicious cycle.

We also have cultural influences that affect how assertive we feel we can be. In many societies, women are supposed to be quiet and docile, and for them to express themselves assertively would be a faux pas. It can be hard to figure out how to handle assertiveness when the underlying factor keeping one from asserting themselves is cultural. Unfortunately, how to deal with this is beyond the scope of this book.

In Western society, assertiveness and being self-assured is not only valued but also encouraged, at least on the surface.

Assertiveness vs. Aggression

As we noted in the chapter opening, assertiveness differs from being aggressive. Aggressive people dominate others around them and act out when that domination is challenged. Assertive people simply make sure their needs are met, and their feelings are expressed.

Aggressive people rarely have much regard for the surrounding people. They want what they want and will do what they need to get it, even at the expense of someone else. If they don't get their way, they are likely to act out in an unhinged manner. The assertive person has a lot of regard for the people around them and takes both themselves and others into consideration before speaking or acting.

There is a tendency for an overly aggressive person to become a bully. Here is another key difference between someone who is aggressive and assertive. The aggressive person is a bully, whereas the assertive person is seeking not to be bullied.

Becoming More Self-Assertive

Of all the things we ask people to do to cultivate self-esteem, understanding and accepting yourself and being more self-assertive tend to the most difficult steps. People who are not used to expressing or speaking up for themselves find it doesn't come naturally and must be forced for a while, if not forever.

You must have confidence to be assertive about your feelings and your needs. Working on developing your self-confidence, which we explore in-depth in the next chapter, is part of developing the ability to be self-assertive when necessary.

Just a quick example is confidence in your beliefs. Until you have confidence that you understand your views and beliefs and have the data and evidence back it, you will have a hard time convincing someone else that you are right. If you aren't even sure about what you are saying, why should someone believe it?

We can't let others decide how we feel about something or shape our opinions; otherwise, they aren't our own. This requires us to take control of our own feelings or emotions, which also means we must value ourselves enough not to care if someone disagrees with us on something we feel strongly about.

Being self-assertive also requires us to value other people more than an overly nice person does. This might sound harsh, but we do have to accept that when we tell others what they want to hear, we are lying to them, which indicates a lack of value we place on them, even if we don't mean to.

If you value someone, you will want to tell him or her the whole truth, even if it hurts or makes you uncomfortable. You must let someone know who you are, and if you hide your opinions behind constant agreement or platitudes, then they don't know you. When someone you care about hurts you, you should want to tell them about it so they can grow and hopefully not do whatever it is again. If you don't tell them, you deny them the opportunity to grow and become better to you.

A solid and healthy relationship requires honest and active participation from both parties.

Becoming more self-assertive means developing courage— courage in your convictions and in your worth. This is, of course, far easier said than done, but it clearly takes personal courage to tell the truth and ask for what we want or need. Conversations and relationships require us to be vulnerable. While this is uncomfortable, it is a vital part of happy, deep relationships. It takes guts and courage to go into an emotionally charged situation, willing to bare your soul, but the results will be good even if it isn't readily apparent at first.

Many people don't even know where to begin when it comes to being more self-assertive. One way to become more assertive and more effective in communication is to take possession of emotions. Say someone insults you. Rather than saying something like "that was mean," take ownership and try something like, "I was hurt when you said that."

It also helps to focus on the behavior rather than the person expressing the behavior. Usually it isn't the person themselves that makes you upset, but rather, their *actions*. So, focus on the action rather than making it personal. They are less likely to respond defensively if you address the behavior so it makes it about the action and doesn't treat it as a personal failing or character flaw.

We also need to discuss the importance of letting the other person have time to understand. After you have asserted yourself, you must allow the person time to change or respond. You can't expect them to act immediately, and if you do, you are being unfair and are not likely to get a positive result.

You must be present and observant in your life and relationships so you can see where you are failing and where you are allowing others to control your life. You must know yourself well enough to know what you want and need before you can ask for it. Perhaps most important, believe that you have a right to an opinion and a say in what happens in your life and your place in the world. None of this is easy, but we wouldn't have so many people dealing with self-esteem issues if it were.

Being assertive doesn't mean always getting your way. Rather, it is a balance between what you need and what others need, as opposed to solely being about what others need. It isn't selfish to consider yourself in a situation that directly affects you. The important part is that both your and others' needs are addressed and considered equally. You aren't trying to "win" or have your opinion dominate the conversation; you just want to be a part of the conversation and have your needs or concerns addressed. It's about being part of the conversation, not taking it over. Again, this is a key difference between being assertive and aggressive.

Chapter 7: Self-Esteem and Pop Culture

Celebrity and pop culture are part of society, whether we like it or not. Though it is easy to see where too much focus on celebrity culture could lead to self-esteem issues, using social media and its connection with self-esteem issues is just getting quality research. With celebrity, it's hard to compete with the looks, money, and material success celebrities have, and if we use this as our measuring stick for our own success, chances are our self-esteem will suffer.

The biggest problem with both celebrity and social media is not that they exist, per se; it is more that too many of us use them as a comparison for our own success, worth, and value to the world. Celebrity culture and social media are often far from reality, which makes the comparison inherently unfair.

Whether we should or not, we make comparisons between others and ourselves. The biggest issue is whom we use as our comparison group. Before the advent of social media, we were more limited to basic celebrity culture and our peer group - our friends, family, coworkers, neighbors, etc. Comparisons between more everyday people and ourselves tend to give us a better indication of our own level of success as it relates to society. We do not get this when our biggest social comparison group is social media-related.

Social media and pop culture dominate our lives to a large extent. How many of us go for more than a few hours without checking social media? We even live in a time where actual important world news may be broken via social media, so eliminating it from our lives isn't necessarily an option, but we can alter how we look at social media and the way we use it.

There is nothing wrong with simply enjoying the glitz and glamor of celebrity culture or even social media personalities we enjoy following. Except, it is helpful to remember that what we see in these spaces is carefully cultivated and isn't unfiltered reality like we might at first think. There are healthy ways to enjoy celebrity culture and social media, but too often, we let it have a negative impact on what we think about ourselves and the value or interest of our own lives. Behold, this is where the problem lies.

We should point out that not all celebrity culture and social media are bad. Like anything, these things can be either good or bad, depending on how we use them and the value we place on it. There are also campaigns for body positivity and celebrities who invite us into their lives to see it isn't as glamorous as it might first appear and that they deal with real everyday problems just like everyone else.

One of the biggest problems is so many of us don't see how much of what we see on social media is an illusion.

Social Media Reality vs. Actual Reality

Most of us spend at least part of our day browsing social media. We are exposed to tons of content, news, some from people like us, and some from people who seem to live charmed and glamorous lives. Some content can be uplifting and inspire us to take chances or to change our lives, but a lot of the content seems to make us feel worse about ourselves.

Look at all these people who are prettier than you, more successful than you, or live more interesting lives. What do they have, and what is wrong with you that you *don't?* Too many of us go through this when we become mired in social media, and it makes it hard for us to be satisfied with ourselves and where we are in life. There will always be someone more successful or exciting than us, and it is detrimental to our mental health to feel bad we can't keep up.

Just think about it. Spending your day looking into the lives of people who seem smarter, happier, more successful, richer, more attractive, or more talented than you can be inspirational only for so long before it makes you feel as though you are lacking. Why aren't you as attractive, as smart or as interesting as social media personalities you like to follow? What do you lack?

But you lack nothing. It helps to remember just how contrived social media and celebrity culture is. Almost none of the content we see from these people is organic. They had makeup artists and wardrobe help them get their look just right. They have professional photographers that help them stage their photos just right. Plus, that amazing "candid" shot you just liked might have been the 20th take of the picture attempt.

The point is that *this isn't reality.* It is staged and framed to make the surroundings look perfect and luxurious than they are. We all want to put ourselves in the best possible light, and celebrities are no different; they just have more money and tools to make this happen than the rest of us.

Staged photos, stylists, carefully framed shots, and extensive filters and editing go into most of what we see online. The point of harping on this is to show this is not reality; it is an illusion of what someone wants to represent his or her reality to be. Sadly, if you believe that everything you see online is real and organic then you are sorely mistaken.

Most people don't show the mundane or bleaker parts of life, especially celebrities and social media influencers that are trying to maintain a persona. There is a fine line between finding this content motivating and this content distressing because it makes us feel less than. A lot of time, being mired in this content will make us feel bad about ourselves because we are not as talented, attractive, or successful as the people we look up to and follow.

Celebrities and influencers seem perpetually happy, busy, and living the best life, which can make someone scrolling through social media in their pajamas while eating popcorn feel bad about himself or herself. We feel like failures in the face of these seemingly perfect people who are always happy and always on the go, doing something far more exciting than what we do.

We don't see them dealing with dog poop or dirty laundry, and although celebrities largely have people who will do these things for them, it isn't like every part of their life is picture-perfect, or that they get out of bed with flawless makeup and clothing. They are presenting an image, and that image leaves a lot out while adding a lot of fake in. To a far lesser extent, many of us also do this when we post online, so we should just expect this from anyone on social media or in celebrity culture. They are trying to sell a product, even if that product is the envy of their lifestyle.

In American society, particularly, celebrity culture has been elevated to an high level. People with few skills or redeeming qualities can become overnight celebrities thanks to reality television and social media. We are shown these people live charmed lives far more interesting and action-packed than our own, and we look at our own lives as if they should be more like television.

And we also have a tendency to fetishize wealth and look at people with more money than we could ever dream of as if they are the model we should aspire to and measure our own success against - no matter how unrealistic or unattainable this might prove to be. Capitalism has allowed for the creation of many success stories, but there are also stories of failure or potential not met that we don't hear about because they don't make good news stories.

But it's motivating to know that other people fail and experience doubt and basic life frustrations just like you. When all we see is a happy, idealized version of someone's life, it can give us the false sense that something about them makes them immune from negative feelings and that frustrations aren't something they have to deal with because they are more or "better."

So much of the value we place on ourselves is based on how we feel we stack up against other people. Constantly comparing ourselves to celebrities and social media influencers is bound to make us feel like we are lesser or lacking. When we use these people as our guide for our own success, happiness, and value, social media and consumption of celebrity culture become negative factors for our self-esteem. There will always be some hot new star that is young, beautiful and seems to have it all. It isn't easy to see, but it is important to know that much of this is simply a presentation; it *isn't reality.*

It is natural to compare oneself to others. In the past, we might have marginally looked at celebrities and thought about what charmed lives they lived, but we seemed to understand this was unattainable and not something most of us can strive for. Much of our self-comparison was with other people in our community including our friends, family, and neighbors. Most of which are on roughly the same material level as us, and thus, more realistic comparisons of our own relative success in the material world.

Fast forward to today, and we are no longer comparing ourselves with our neighbors or that guy in class you are always trying to edge out for best grade. Rather, we are comparing ourselves to celebrities, wealthy personalities, and social media influencers with a ton of money, equipment, and means to make their lives look far more exciting than we could ever hope for.

This is called the upward comparison, and when done modestly, it can be motivating for us to take risks and try more. But when that is the only comparison, it is easy to see how we can quickly feel bad about ourselves. We can't stack up against wealthy celebrities with a team of people who help keep them looking as good as humanly possible whenever they are in public.

It is a huge mistake to consider what we see on social media to be real life and use it to measure the value of our own lives. As we already noted, most of what you see on social media and especially in celebrity magazines is highly filtered, posed, and, well, *contrived.* It isn't reality; it is a *well-crafted illusion.*

Self-presentation is a huge part of social media, and we all try to make ourselves look good most of the time. For example, even regular folks will move a pile of dirty laundry out of a picture, so it looks like their surroundings are perfect and far less cluttered than they are. It's helpful to understand how even we present a false picture of ourselves when we use social media since we, too, try to frame ourselves and our pictures in the best light.

If you are experiencing confidence issues, it's helpful to look closely at your social media usage. Is social media the biggest benchmark you use for comparison? What types of people do you follow? If you spend much of your social time using social media and follow very few "regular people," chances are your experience isn't always positive. It can be fun and even inspiring to look at the lives of those with a lot more than you, but this can't be the only group you have to compare yourself. You also must remember just how much of what you see is manufactured.

Negative Effects of Social Media

Social media not only takes up a lot of our time, but there is also a lot of new research that shows those of us who use social media a lot may be more likely to have mental health issues than those who are only casual users. Chou and Edge performed a study in 2012 that showed that frequent Facebook users tend to think others are happier and more successful than themselves.

But when we compare ourselves to what we see on social media, it is like comparing our actual real life, with all its mess, to a carefully crafted, idealized presentation. Basically, it is an unfair and unrealistic comparison, but many of us fall into this trap. Unfortunately, it can have very negative impacts on how we view our value to the world and ourselves in general.

Even when interacting with people closer to being peers in terms of material success and the like, we often use arbitrary and useless measures that mean nothing to compare ourselves with them. For example, how many followers does someone have compared to you? How many likes do their pictures get versus yours? We all do this, but it is silly when you think about it. There are inorganic ways of getting likes and follows, and it doesn't matter. Numbers do not affect value or worth. We shouldn't base our usefulness or value on statistics like this, but we do, all too often.

It seems that the more immersed we are in celebrity and social media culture, the more likely it is to have a negative impact on our self-esteem and overall mental health. Studies by Feinstein and others in 2013 showed that people who use social media excessively report higher depression rates and a lower sense of wellbeing.

Chronic social media users are also likely to report lower levels of self-esteem than casual users, indicating a correlation between the amount of time we spend in the virtual space and our sense of wellbeing. This is likely because, in the virtual space, we are more likely to engage in upward social comparison with people with things we can never hope to have. Chronic users are constantly exposed to people who seem "better" than they are, and this can naturally have negative effects on how they feel about themselves.

Some people are better at moderating their social media usage than others and can easily limit themselves with things like screen time monitors. Other people can't do this, and to get out of that trap, we might have to spend time away from social media to ensure that we don't let it take over our lives and become negative to our overall wellbeing and self-esteem.

Positive Elements of Social Media

When used casually and with the right mindset, social media is a fun distraction and can even motivate at times. It can be a great way to blow off steam or interact with people who share the same interests. The problem isn't social media itself, so much as using this virtual space as our primary means for self-comparison with others. We discussed earlier that it is far less "real" than we might originally think.

As much as we have focused on negative aspects of social media, there are also motivating and uplifting elements of it and celebrity culture. We have recently seen a lot more body positive content, including the rise of plus-size models that give us something beyond the stick-thin Barbie to aspire to. Body positivity aims to help regular people feel better about their imperfect selves and give people better, more realistic role models.

This is a good thing for many reasons. Foremost, most of us can't aspire to look like a runway model. Those people must work exceptionally hard for their bodies, and it can be a full-time job to look the way they do. People come in all shapes and sizes, and beauty isn't one-size-fits-all. We can strive to become healthier versions of ourselves, but we also must accept what our body looks like to some extent. Especially for younger generations, not having any role models that look like normal people can have detrimental effects, so any furthering of body positivity is good for current and future generations.

More brands are coming out with plus size clothing and using models of all shapes and sizes in their advertising, which is a good thing. This gives us more than one "shape" of the body that is the one we should strive for. It helps us feel like we are okay as we are, even if we aren't tall and thin like the Victoria Secret models. The rise in more plus size clothing options provides more inclusivity, and even higher-end brands such as Rihanna's Savage X Fenty now offer plus sizes, which is not something we would have seen even just a few years ago.

For a long time, bigger people were limited in the clothes available to them. They were frumpy and not at all what was in fashion, which went further to making plus-sized people feel like something was wrong with them. Seeing more brands offer cutting edge plus-size trends, and more luxury brands also expanding their offerings goes a long way towards both self-acceptance and societal acceptance of a multitude of beauty standards.

Some celebrities are using social media to help break the idea of a "perfect star" with a charmed life and no problems. They are letting people into the darker and messier parts of their lives by sharing their battles with mental illness or even difficult pregnancies. This might not seem like much, but with all the sanitized and artificial content we typically consume, hearing celebrities who seem so much "more" than us talking about problems we deal with can help bring them down from the pedestal we placed them on and make them seem more like regular people with real-life problems.

In recent years, social media has raised concerns about mental health, body image, and more. Men's mental health and body positivity are finally starting to get notice and attention, which is great. While women face a lot of beauty and other standards, men to face these. They are told they shouldn't be emotional and that it is a character flaw if they struggle with mental issues. We are seeing this paradigm shift, which is wonderful, since we all need to feel comfortable and okay with asking for help when we need it. Needing help is part of being human. It is starting to be "okay" for a man to seek mental health care, but there is still a stigma largely attached to it.

Many men "aren't okay" and would benefit from mental health services but have been made to feel as if they are showing weakness or are lesser men if they ask for help. So many tragedies and lives of quiet depression could be avoided if people felt as if it were okay to ask for help when they needed it. These campaigns aimed at men are trying to normalize the idea that sometimes men need help too, and there is nothing to be ashamed of. This is a sadly deeply engrained idea likely to take generations to work out.

While different, men, too, deal with issues of body image. Just think about the "quintessential man"; he is young and fit with a full head of hair. You get the idea. Like with the stereotypical "perfect woman," very few men fit these standards, and it affects self-esteem and feelings of self-worth. Body positivity for men, women, non-binary people is a good thing for our mental health all around, and we hope this trend continues.

We have also seen more age-positive content. Social media and celebrity culture focus on youth, and as we age, it can seem like we become less and less important to society. Older celebrities and even social media personalities are opening up about aging and their feelings surrounding it and the unique challenges they face as stars when they age. This can help us feel empowered by our age, rather than ashamed, which is important in our youth-driven celebrity culture.

Basically, celebrities have been letting us into their lives behind all the illusion to see what they are like. They get pimples, experience setbacks, and have issues. Because we look up to them so much, there can be something empowering about discovering that your favorite celebrity has also dealt with doubt and sought help in the process. If even they need those kinds of things, how can we fault ourselves as "mere mortals" for needing it as well?

Finally, untouched photos and those free of filters have become a "thing" among celebrities and social media influencers. These are actually real pictures, not ones staged and filtered to perfection. Celebrities are sharing pictures of themselves without makeup, with bedhead, and in other real-life situations we can relate to because, well, they are real. This helps break the stereotype that people who live "better" than we don't suffer from basic irritations of life and perhaps, at times, don't look perfect.

We have a lot of hope these trends will continue, and transparency becomes more the norm. We can tell you until we are blue in the face that celebrities and social media personalities are just humans with their own issues and faults, but if you never see it but constantly see your own, it's hard to believe this. As they allow us into their real lives, showing us the good and the bad, social media usage becomes a little less problematic as it jives more with reality than an idealized version of it.

It's hard to find that balance between healthy social media usage and consumption of celebrity culture and using it so much and in such a way it has a detrimental impact on our life and our feelings. When used casually, it can be a fun distraction or allow us to interact with people who share our interests. Occasionally looking at celebrity content can even have a motivating factor for some of us.

The big thing is keeping everything in perspective. Often, what is on social media is engineered and, well, not actual reality. Celebrities don't roll out of bed looking perfect and don't leave the gym looking flawless without effort. A lot of behind-the-scenes work goes into what seems like candid photos or content we often forget about. It is an illusion of reality, not actual reality.

It is also important to limit the amount of upward comparison we do when thinking about how we stack up against others. Looking up to highly successful people isn't a bad thing but when this is the only social group we use for comparison, it can have a negative impact on our lives. We must be realistic with our social comparisons. We will get a much better idea of what our lives look like to others when we compare ourselves with the person down the street than the latest big Hollywood celeb. Better still would be to stop comparing ourselves to others, which we will look at in the next chapter.

Chapter 8: Start Building Your Confidence

In a variety of ways, we have shown how important it is to have self-confidence, but for those lacking confidence, gaining it doesn't come naturally or easily. It is easy to tell people they need more confidence; however, this doesn't help them or tell them anything they don't already know. Most people lacking in self-confidence are perfectly aware of this lacking; they just aren't sure how to fix it.

We can do a lot of things that will help us begin to look at ourselves with more kindness and gain a sense of confidence that allows us to take more control over our lives, wants, and needs. Though it must first be stated: no one thing works for everyone, and this requires effort. For people telling themselves for years they aren't worthy and don't matter, it takes a lot more than a positive mantra to make them believe and internalize this.

The ability to trust our own judgment and abilities is important in many areas of life. Having confidence allows us to ask for what we need and results in better careers and more meaningful interpersonal relationships. Self-confidence is important because it enables us to have the courage to take risks, express our emotions, or ask for what we want or need in life. Sadly, for people with low self-esteem, confidence is severely lacking or even nonexistent, and changing this doesn't happen overnight.

It is important for both our physical and mental wellbeing to have a healthy level of self-confidence. Confidence can make you more willing to try new things and consider taking on challenges that might prove very meaningful or fruitful for your life. It also helps you become a better communicator, as you are more self-assured when it comes to the worth of your wants, needs, feelings, and ideas. Lacking self-confidence makes so many things a struggle that can, in turn, reinforce negative self-feelings, that turn into an ugly, self-perpetuating cycle of negativity.

How to Improve Your Confidence

One of the first things we need to do to boost our confidence concerns social comparisons. As discussed in the chapter on social media and celebrity culture, too much upward social comparison can cause negative impacts on our self-outlook because we are giving ourselves an unreasonable comparison. We can take this further, though, because we really shouldn't be comparing ourselves to others as it is.

We are not only all different, but we are also at different stages in life, and we have different goals and abilities. This can make comparing one person to another like comparing apples to oranges - we are not comparing the same things, and thus the comparison isn't helpful. It might seem like it's motivating to try to compete with others and use them as our standard for comparison; it also reduces our confidence and may even make us less sure of our own skill and ability.

Though this seems obvious, we are not other people. They haven't had the same life experience. They don't have the same inner mentality. They do not have the skills or challenges we have. We have had a unique experience and are unique creatures that really shouldn't be compared with other unique creatures with different circumstances and situations than our own.

We should be our comparisons, not anyone else. There is a fine line between envy and the way we ultimately feel about ourselves, and when we remove those upward comparisons and use ourselves as our measure of how far we've come in life, we get a much more accurate picture. Life isn't a competition anyway. When looking at ourselves, we should be thinking about how far we have come in our life's journey, the obstacles we have overcome, the challenges we have met, and how we can leverage our skills and abilities to better improve our lives.

Another important part of developing self-confidence and a positive outlook requires self-care. We must take care of ourselves physically, mentally, and spiritually if we want to live our best lives. We have stated this multiple times and will discuss it again, but if you aren't taking care of yourself, it is hard to feel good about anything. You will not feel great physically, and you probably won't like what you see when you look in the mirror if you ignore your own health and wellbeing.

We must address our personal needs if we want to be happy, healthy, and successful people. Our bodies need proper sleep, food, hydration, activity, and personal time. Things like a physical activity not only help us look and feel better physically, but it can also help improve our mood and overall mental wellbeing, which can make it easier to gain confidence about oneself.

Again, we must state something that should be obvious but may not be—practicing self-care is not selfish; it is reasonable and responsible.

Having compassion for ourselves will also help us become more accepting of ourselves and will help us our journey to boost our self-confidence. We must give ourselves a break. We aren't perfect. Nobody is perfect. There will never be a perfect human. And that's okay! Everybody experiences failure, shame, embarrassment, and disappointment. It is okay to feel these emotions, but we should try to feel them with tenderness, the way we would look at the misfortune of someone we love.

We need to work towards speaking more kindly to ourselves, especially when we are down. Kindness is more motivating for most of us than constant negative self-talk. For many, these constant feelings of lacking act as a barrier, stopping them from moving forward with any aspect of their life and thus contributing to more negative feelings about themselves.

Everyone experiences failure. Everyone. Having a setback is not an indictment of your value or worth to society; it is a human experience we all must face. Again, try to give yourself a break and look at yourself the way you would look at your closest friend who just suffered a setback. Being able to treat ourselves with compassion and care will help us understand that we deserve to feel our feelings but also, that we are not "the worst" because we made a mistake.

Self-doubt is something that even the most successful person deals with, but the big difference is that they address the doubt and then move on. Doubt is a normal part of the human experience and can be a good thing since it makes us look more closely at our decisions and get advice or feedback from others that can help us make better choices. It is okay to have doubt - in fact, it would be an issue if we never had any - but the problem arises when we let this doubt keep us from trying or acting.

Acting, even if you fail, can often improve confidence because you TRIED. Trying is a huge deal. It takes a ton of courage, and even in failure, there is a lot to learn if we are willing. Prepare, practice, but don't let the fear of failure stop you from trying. You'll never be 100% confident about most things, and life will always have some doubt. But we must learn how to harness and control this doubt so it can guide our choices but not let it control us and keep us from even attempting something.

You will also need to challenge yourself (not that what we have discussed isn't challenging, of course). We mean that when you engage in negative self-talk, you need to challenge that self-talk. Address that negative inner critic and engage it. Tell the voice is wrong and just trying to hold you back. It is irrational, and you will not keep listening to it.

Our negative thoughts are often wrong, and if we probe them a little, that will become plain to see. Looking at our inner critic more closely will let us better determine when it has legitimate criticism and when it is irrational.

Actionable Steps Towards Self-Confidence

A lot of what we have talked about so far is rather abstract, but it is vitally important for developing healthy levels of self-confidence. One great way to start on this journey to improved self-confidence is to list all the achievements and strengths you have, no matter how small. Seriously, list everything, even if you are listing something as seemingly inconsequential as being a good whistler. This list should show you that even where you are right now, you have a lot of strengths.

Refer back to this list often so you never forget where you've come from and what you have accomplished. Add to this list as you go. As your confidence grows, so too will the strengths we allow ourselves to see.

Though it won't come naturally at first, try to think positively about yourself. Force yourself if necessary. You don't even have to focus on something major; it can be a small thing. Say you made a killer grilled cheese sandwich. Take a minute to pat yourself on the back for what a good job you did. Little things like this will allow you to see that you do positive things and have positive qualities readily apparent if we let ourselves see them.

You will want to set realistic challenges for yourself for raising your self-confidence. This can be as simple as making yourself say positive daily mantras or taking a few minutes to journal about the positive aspects of your day. The more you surround yourself with positivity, the more it will positively affect your overall mood and your wellbeing. Setting tiny goals, such as making sure you get proper hydration for a week, then achieving said goal, can go a long way in helping to improve self-confidence. When you see yourself reaching these goals, it is hard to feel bad about yourself.

Again, you will want to make sure you are engaging in self-care since when we look and feel good, it will often affect your mental outlook.

Do you have a list of things you've always wanted to do? Dust off that list and reconsider it. What on the list is realistic or attainable? Make a new list with these realistic goals, add any you can think of, and make a real plan as to how to achieve these goals.

It can also be helpful to evaluate your social circle and involve them in your efforts to improve your self-confidence. You need a social network of supportive people who see the good in you, not people who bring you down or make you feel like everything is a competition. Consciously practice kindness with yourself and others, even if it doesn't feel natural. Over time, it will become part of who you are, and you can do this without giving it much thought.

Chapter 9: How to Live with Purpose

For most people, meaning and purpose are what they are looking for in life, but many of us have no idea how to do this. Feeling like we are just floating through life on autopilot is not a good feeling, and it isn't surprising that since so many of us do this because we have issues with self-esteem and feelings of self-worth. Nobody likes to feel as if they have no control in their life, and it's hard to find a purpose in a life not controlled by you.

We have discussed numerous times how you can take back control of your life, feelings, and opinions, so we won't go into detail about it here. We all want our lives to be fulfilling and to give us a sense that we are involved with something bigger than ourselves. This seems to be a common human goal across the ages and across cultures. So why is it so difficult?

Life is busy; we work, we have obligations, and perhaps we have children too. This can make us feel like we are pulled in so many directions while we never even stop to think about the purpose or meaning of our life, but we also live with the vague sense of being unfulfilled.

If we are brave enough to do what is needed to take control of our lives, we have a lot of choice in how we live them. Too many of us live our lives based on what we think society wants from us, which, in effect, takes control of our own existence away from us and puts it into the hands of this vague concept of "societal norms." Being unhappy and unsatisfied with our lives makes us feel bad, out of control, and can become a vicious cycle of self-doubt and self-hatred.

While it isn't easy and will take time, you can take that control over your life back and live with meaning and purpose. It will take time. It involves figuring out what you value, believe, and what is important in life. How can these values be used to help further the greater good? No matter what you think is important, whether it be adult literacy or concern about stray animals and their well-being, there are ways you can make this value a driving force in your life.

What is Involved in a Meaningful Life?

The world was here before us and will continue on after us, and this can make us feel inconsequential and meaningless, but when we find ways to connect ourselves to causes or ideas that are bigger than ourselves and will continue on after we are gone, we can start to feel like we are part of something with far greater meaning and value than one human life.

This "bigger purpose" is something that we may spend much, if not all, our lives searching for. We need something that will enrich us mentally and spiritually, that we also feel to value for the future and is addressing an issue or cause that will affect lives far beyond just our own.

We live beyond ourselves when we participate in movements that affect not just our lives but those of generations to come. This is why so many people who feel as if they live purposeful and meaningful lives are part of causes bigger than themselves and that they feel will have a positive impact on society.

Whether we like animals, are concerned about social justice, or are passionate about STEM fields being more prominent in public schools, we all have an interest in something with an effect on more than just us and can contribute to the greater good. Getting involved with movements or activities like this will help us feel like we are part of the greater society, doing things that positively contribute to our future.

Many people feel as if they find their "calling" when they get involved in a movement or organization that tackles an important issue. It can also be rewarding to help others struggling to find their calling. Not only will this make you feel good about yourself; it can help other people.

When you are involved with something you are passionate about, it doesn't feel like work, and it feels like you have found a home. This sense of purpose and meaning has a value that cannot be quantified.

We can also help ourselves live a life with meaning and purpose by engaging in life with love and self-confidence. This, of course, is a lot easier said than done. Having something in your life, like a cause that makes you feel engaged with something larger than yourself, can help you find greater levels of self-esteem, as you feel engrossed with life and part of the group so it is hard to find anywhere else. When we do something for the greater good, it becomes much harder to tell ourselves that we are lacking or unworthy of love and respect.

Benefits of a Purposeful Life

It might seem like living a life of meaning and purpose is self-evident, good, and that is correct, but the benefits of living a meaningful life go beyond just making it easier to convince us we have value and are deserving of a good life.

When we feel like we are living meaningful lives, the normal pitfalls of everyday life can become easier to bear. Those who are involved in causes or organizations that give them a sense of purpose often report they have an easier time dealing with and moving on from disappointment and failure. It becomes easier to let go of ill will towards others and yourself and to move on from negative elements of your past.

When our lives have meaning, we learn how to better embrace life and live with gratitude and compassion. We spend our time engaged in good and beneficial behavior. When life feels like it has value and meaning, we can expand our mental horizons and gain empathy, which helps us accept ourselves and makes us more accepting of others. We learn to better understand others' actions and feelings, which is beneficial for all involved because it makes us better communicators and friends.

We all have a system of values and beliefs, even if we have spent little time thinking about them. This is the time to think about what you feel and believe; what you think brings value to your life. When you know what you value and think, you can live more in accordance with those values.

Living a purposeful life also requires you to have realistic goals and set realistic priorities. We should spend as much time as we possibly can on activities that further our value and provide good to the world at large, but it is important not to overdo it. We must have balance in our lives. Just like we need a good work/life balance, we also need balance in our efforts to make the world a better place. We aren't much use to the world if we are exhausted and malnourished.

Living a life of meaning requires us to be present at the moment and to pay attention to what is going on around us. This can also help us reduce distraction and to pay more attention to our internal needs.

Man's search for meaning and purpose is a quest as old as mankind itself, and it is often a lifelong process. Viktor Frankl, an influential Austrian psychologist, said that finding meaning in our existence is one of our life's defining forces, even if we aren't actively aware of this. We can give meaning and purpose to our lives, depending on what matters to us, our abilities, and where our values lie.

On a personal level, knowing and living by your values is not just a generally meaningful life, but a life with personal purpose. On a bigger-picture level, we look to be part of something that goes beyond our short time on this earth. For most of us, the big picture purpose will involve giving. That might mean giving time, love, thought, or even money.

Those who have found purpose are happier than those who feel like their life lacks meaning. They also have confidence and are surer of themselves. Since we all seek meaning and purpose, as Frankl noted, this is a very human journey that might be the ultimate expression of what it means to be a human.

Some people find their meaning and calling early in life, but many of us aren't that lucky. We can know that what we are doing is giving us meaning and purpose when work doesn't feel like work. Instead, it feels like a hobby or another form of personal enrichment. Your actions start to become an extension of your values, and you will often lose yourself in the work because it is some immersive to your very being.

Sometimes, especially if we are struggling to find a meaning or purpose, we need to pull back from our daily life. Breaking out of routine drudgery is also necessary. We have to figure out who we are, where our values lie, and what is truly important for us if we want to find ways to live a life filled with meaning and purpose.

Chapter 10: Meditation as a Mindful Practice

Meditation has long been a daily part of life for billions of people, especially for those from Eastern cultures. It has continued to gain popularity in recent decades and is now even commonly practiced by many people throughout the West. There is a good reason for this, as this ancient practice is invaluable to countless people across space and time.

Meditation is one of the most important of the mindfulness practices. Mindfulness simply refers to the ability to be mindful of and live in the moment. It is taking the time to observe your surroundings, inner feelings and live life more deliberately and with greater gratitude and purpose. Because of what is involved in the practice, meditation helps get you in the here and now and provides the ability to help you find mental clarity, reduce stress, and find greater value and purpose in life.

It is helpful to calm your mind and allow yourself to get rid of the inconsequential thoughts that inundate us daily. We must remove ourselves from the hustle and bustle and steal moments for us to just be and to just experience the present as a means to manage the stresses of the future better.

Before we get into how to meditate, we need to make a huge forewarning: meditation is HARD. It isn't easy. It is difficult. Any other way of something not coming naturally, you need to illustrate the point. Being in the moment with our minds still and calm is almost the antithesis of modern society, and being creatures of modern society, it is hard to remove ourselves from the mindset we always need to go, go, go.

Meditation takes practice, and for many people, it is years before, if they ever, learn to master the practice. If you find meditation difficult, good, that means you are in good company. Most people do, which is why it takes years to master. The effort is worth it as we get value from the mere practice of meditation, even if it isn't as successful as we would like it to be.

The Science of Meditation

Many people swear by meditation, a practice used by millions for centuries, but is there any science to back up the claims of its benefits? It turns out there actually is. We should note this has been studied for decades, and there is promising current research that is ongoing, but there are difficulties with this type of research due to the nature of what we are seeking to understand. We will discuss this more below.

There have been several studies into the value and efficacy of many mindfulness practices, but meditation is one of the most important.

One thing science has shown us is that the practice of meditation helps us with our attention. If we have short attention spans, it can help us hold our focus for longer. It helps us stay present, so we are open and aware of new information and stimuli that we might often ignore out of habit.

Evidence shows that the long-term practice of meditation can reduce overall stress levels. This isn't to say that people who meditate never experience stress, but rather that they experience it at lower rates and appear to be much better suited in dealing with stress in a healthy manner. It appears that the process of meditation allows us to slow down and process things in a healthier manner, to have a clearer mind, which can make us more adaptable to changes.

Research from prominent educational institutions has also shown that meditation can help reduce the effects of certain health conditions from irritable bowel syndrome to fibromyalgia, but there should be some caution in taking too much from these studies just yet. There have been complaints about the methodology used or the small sample sizes employed in these studies, which could affect the ability to generalize these results to the population.

More rigorous and randomized controlled studies are now being used to make more sense of this data and determine how much value we can place on the results. There are issues that will make any research on this subject difficult, and part of it is the subjective nature of the phenomena we wish to study.

One of the biggest problems facing researchers is common — small sample sizes. The larger a sample population you can use in your study, the more likely it will generally apply to society. Many of the studies conducted have fewer than 100 participants, and these participants' demographics may not represent society as a whole. Commonly, this can limit what can be gleaned from these studies.

Another difficulty is the ambiguity in the definition of terms like mindfulness and the many types of meditation practiced. Who is to say that one type of meditation isn't superior to others? When we say participants in a study practiced meditation, what kind of mediation? In what setting did they practice and for how long? As you can see, the variety of types of practice, and the slippery nature of a definition of mindfulness, has made this a pretty difficult area of study.

Recent research from Harvard also shows there may be positive benefits for depressed individuals who practice meditation. This is not a "miracle cure." Studies have shown there is a moderate positive effect for people who practice meditation, but it will not take the place of medication or therapy. Rather, it is just one more tool in our therapeutic arsenal for dealing with stress and depression.

Studies and reviews of studies show evidence that the practice of mediation may have tangible effects on our brain and its functioning. There are current studies underway by the NCCIH into the effects of meditation on chronic pain, stress reduction in people with a range of specific conditions, and how it can affect ailments like headaches or reduce blood pressure.

This exciting research could give much more credence to the claims of positive therapeutic outcomes related to meditation and could lead to it becoming more widely used as a treatment among the mainstream medical community. We look forward to the results and what they can tell us about this ancient practice.

Besides the development of more scientific research, we have centuries of people noting the positive effect it has on their lives. Though we may not understand the mechanisms that underlie it, there are many tangible, positive benefits to the practice of meditation as people have sworn by its value for hundreds of years. People, who have practiced meditation for long periods, often report better handling stress and frustration, better concentration, can live in the moment, and more. It might be hard to quantify this in a scientific study, but it isn't hard for us to see how these things could be incredibly beneficial in daily life.

How to Meditate

The first thing you must do is find a clean, quiet place free from distractions. This might be a place in your house or even an outdoor location. You want privacy, so you aren't interrupted, and keep electronics out of the area unless you are using them for guided mediation or if you want to play soft, ambient music to help quiet outside noise you can't avoid and might cause distraction.

We cannot stress enough how important blocking out distraction is. If you cannot focus yourself on your practice, you will not get as much out of it as you could. It might be difficult for you to find a place in your home suitable for meditation, so consider outside areas. If you can get a few quiet minutes alone in your backyard or garden, this might be the best meditation spot for you.

You should be comfortable when you meditate. This includes the clothes you wear and how you sit. Most people wear loose, comfortable clothes. Meditation most often takes place seated on the floor, but you can sit on a pad or cushion to make this more comfortable. You don't have to wear exercise clothes; your everyday clothes will be fine. All that is required is that you wear something comfortable that won't distract you or make you uncomfortable during practice.

You want your body to be relaxed and comfortable, and not all of us can do the quintessential meditation pose for long periods of time, so it is a good thing it isn't necessary. The most important thing is to be comfortable and sit in a way that is conducive to deep breathing. You need to be able to take full, deep breaths, as this is a huge part of meditation. Most people meditate seated. You might sit on the floor, on a cushion, or even on a chair. There is no right way to meditate, except to get comfortable.

Before you meditate, you want to think about what you hope to get out of it. Are you looking for inner calm, a way to de-stress, or maybe personal insight? Whatever it is, you need to have your reasoning clear in your mind so you can state your intention and come up with a mantra, or short phrase, that relates to this intention. You will repeat this mantra later during practice.

Once you have stated your intention and know your mantra, close your eyes, and concentrate on your body. What do you feel? Focus closely on these sensations. Then, focus on your breathing. Take slow, dee breaths, focusing on breathing in and breathing out. This will help to focus your mind and relax your body. Do this for as long as you need to to feel yourself relax. This is when you know you are in the right frame of mind.

Once your breathing has become slow and deliberate, focus more closely on your breathing. Now, state your mantra and repeat it in your head. If you find yourself struggling, focus on something or a space in the room and don't take your eyes off it. The idea is to focus so closely on something that your mind becomes free of conscious thought, and you are living purely in the moment. It might take a few sessions for you to do this, but concentrating and focusing on an object or space can be helpful to get in this frame of mind.

Other Advice and Considerations

Though it might seem obvious, in order to get better at mediation, you must meditate! You must do it regularly and avoid taking long breaks between sessions. It will never get easier if you have a variable schedule of practice. You don't have to sit there staring at a wall for hours. Simply spending 10 minutes at a time, three to four times a week, is a great way to get started.

There is no benefit to overdoing it. It will probably lead to more negative issues than positive outcomes. There is also no need to spend hours on end trying to meditate. It isn't a marathon. Clearing your mind isn't something you can do for long durations when you aren't even used to doing it for short periods of time. You may have to try out different locations, using ambient music versus silence, using verbal mantras, or simply saying them in your head. We are all different, and what is most effective for you is what you should stick with. There is no *right way* to meditate.

Once you feel like you have mastered 10 minutes, kick it up to 20. There is really no need to practice for longer than this unless you want to. Some people will increase the number of times a week they practice, as they become more adepts at it.

You must have patience with meditation. As we stated earlier, it isn't easy and especially for those of us who live in urban areas. In the fast-paced Western world, clearing our minds and just sitting still for periods at a time isn't something we are conditioned to do. You are likely to have bad sessions where you can't concentrate or focus your mind. That's okay; you can try again.

If you continue to struggle in meditation, consider trying *guided practice*. This is generally led online, though it can be in person, by an expert at meditation who is there to guide you through the experience and keep you focused on what you need to be.

The great thing about meditation is that it helps to reduce stress and helps improve feelings of general wellbeing. It helps you pay more attention to life so you can appreciate and have gratitude for the little things. It can help you find ways to carve out your time, even in a hectic schedule. Meditation helps you be able to quiet your mind, and it can also make it easier for you to tune out negative thoughts that often cause self-doubt and other negative emotions. There is also evidence it helps to lower blood pressure, making it something that is good for our minds, bodies, and souls.

Regardless of the type of mediation you practice, where you practice, and how you practice it, there is a lot of evidence to support the positive benefits on our overall mental wellbeing. It can help us feel calmer and clearer in our thoughts and feelings. The act of meditation itself gives us a few minutes to take ourselves away from the hustle and bustle of the world and cut out a few moments where we can just be. Doing so can make us more easily able to manage stress or emotionally charged situations and can make it possible for us to unwind our minds, which so many of us need to do in today's stressful world.

It is worth the time and effort it takes to practice, and thankfully, this isn't an expensive practice to pick up. You need nothing except yourself and a cushion. You can easily find help sites online to give you tips on how to improve your meditation, how to get over common pitfalls and to give you mantras you can use in practice if you are studying. There are countless books and videos that will also help you understand the basics of practice.

You can often find guided meditation videos online for free and music carefully curated for use while meditating. Since many of us live in urban areas and don't have a good spot, we can get away from all the noise; having well selected ambient tracks available can be helpful.

Some people participate in group mediation or in-person mediation, and you might be surprised at just how many types of meditation there are. Mediation can be done alone; in groups, there are even walking meditation groups. To go a bit beyond just meditation, consider taking a yoga class in person or online to use meditation techniques in a stretching exercise routine that is also highly beneficial for your body and soul.

Try different types of meditation and practice it in different settings. Try music and try silence. Find what works for you. We are all different, and to get the full benefits of meditation, we must find what works best for us. When you notice that something you have tried has allowed for greater focus, or you feel like you got more out of a session, note it and integrate it into future sessions. You will eventually find a routine that works for you.

Chapter 11: Daily Affirmations

We have mentioned self-mantras and positive affirmations several times throughout this book, but now it is time to look closely at what this actually means and how we can put them into practice.

A positive affirmation is a short mantra or sentence we tell ourselves daily to help reduce stress and boost our self-esteem. It might seem silly, but there is a lot of benefit in giving little pep talks to tell ourselves it will all be okay, that we are worthy, and that we will make it through whatever the day may bring. Many people find this to be helpful, even those who were skeptical at first about the usefulness of positive affirmations.

Self-Affirmation Theory

Self-affirmation theory is a psychological theory that asserts that positive self-affirmation can help us boost our feelings of self-worth and make us feel like we have the potential to meet challenges and achieve goals. When we practice self-affirmation, it becomes part of our personal narrative.

MRI evidence indicates that parts of the brain, including the prefrontal cortex, become more active when we engage in self-affirmation. This part of the brain is associated with information about self and information processing. This indicates that our brain is internalizing these mantras and associating them with the self. Some also believe the self-affirmation can reduce stress.

When we practice self-affirmation, we become more prepared to manage emotionally charged situations and make us more like to practice self-care. Not only can these affirmations help improve our feelings of value and worth, but they can also give us a more generally positive outlook on life, which, in turn, makes us healthier mentally. Some psychologists also recommend the use of positive self-affirmation to get over trauma.

There is also a wealth of personal testimony about the effectiveness of daily positive self-affirmation. They can help put us in the right headspace to face our day with kindness and compassion, both towards others and ourselves. It might feel forced and not genuine at first, but this is common and natural. The more you do it, the more you can internalize what you are saying, and the more you will benefit from it. Many people do this as part of their morning routine to help prepare them for the day's stresses.

Examples of Daily Mantras

Now that we know some science behind the value of positive affirmation let's talk about how this is done and what types of phrases are used in these affirmations. One of the best ways to get the most out of daily affirmations is to use it as a short meditation session with the affirmation as your mantra.

Find a quiet, private place where you can be free of distractions and clear your head. Focus on your breathing, like you do during meditation, until you feel yourself physically relax, and your mind is clear of daily toils.

Next, you want to visualize a peaceful, quiet setting that is the epitome of calm for you. This should include detailed visualization. Think about the sounds, the sights, the smells, and focus on each one of these in turn. Not only will this make you feel good; it is a trick to get daily thoughts and worries out of your mind, so you are making your daily affirmations in a good mental space.

Creating this sense of inner calm helps you start the day more relaxed and may make it easier to internalize and really take to heart the affirmations you speak.

Now that you know what type of environment you need to say your daily affirmations in, let's look at some specific mantras you might choose for yourself.

Inner Health Studios Provides the Following Examples of Positive Affirmations

- I am at peace with myself
- I deserve to be happy
- My future is bright and positive
- I value myself as a person

Jessica DW Offers the Following Affirmations

- I am my best source of motivation
- Everything is possible
- I am compassionate with others and myself
- I appreciate all I have
- All I need is within me
- I attract positive people into my life
- I am stronger than I seem

Life Sorted Offers Mantras as Well Since Not All Mantras are Self-Directed, You Might Consider Ones Intended for Others

- You are powerful
- You should be proud of yourself
- I am limitless

- I love my flaws

- Believe in yourself

Positive Psychology Offers Slightly More Detailed Affirmations

- I believe in myself and trust my own wisdom

- My life is taking place right here, right now

- Nobody but me decides how I feel

- I am confident and capable of what I do

These are just a few examples. You can find countless more at various places online, and there are even books full of affirmations if you are struggling to find one that meets your exact needs. Don't just rely on these though, come up with your own that are personalized and meaningful to you. These phrases and statements can help you guard against negative thoughts that create excessive doubt and erode self-esteem. This should be done regularly, and many do it daily as a part of their self-care routine.

Chapter 12: Applying Self-Care

Self-care is something we have talked about numerous times throughout this book but haven't gone into the outside of a surface glance. Too many of us feel like doing anything good for ourselves is selfish and a luxury we shouldn't need, and this couldn't be farther from the truth. We can hardly live our best lives and offer anything to society if we are exhausted and mentally drained all the time. Nor can we feel great about ourselves if our diet is awful and hygiene is lacking.

Most people don't associate basic self-care with self-esteem, but they absolutely should. Failure to provide proper self-care is a symptom of low self-esteem, to begin with.

Self-care is multifaceted and goes beyond basic care for one's physical needs, though it does also include that. Self-care means care of the body, mind, and soul, not just the body. It isn't always easy to give ourselves the self-care we need since we are busy and pulled in many directions simultaneously. Most of us juggle many life roles: boss, coworker, friend, spouse, parent.

Some of us have been conditioned to think of self-care as selfish when it is vital to us being the best and offering the most to the world around us. What free time many of us do have is taken up by distraction rather than efforts to provide ourselves with the physical and mental nourishment we need.

But self-care shouldn't be something we even have to argue about; it should be obvious this is not only a good thing to do but also a vital thing to do. But we live in a society that sometimes has its priorities out of whack, and many of us believe that we are being selfish or could better use our time if we practice self-care.

Think about the people around you that need you: your family, your children, your coworkers, and your friends. If you cannot practice self-care for yourself, do it for them. They need you to be healthy and around for a long time, and if you continually fail to take care of your basic health and wellness, this might not be possible. We not only have a right, but we must take care of our minds and bodies not only for our own benefit but also to benefit those we love.

Ways to Improve Our Self-Care

There are a lot of ways we can improve our self-care, some more obvious than others. All are important, and while some of these things might not seem like that big of a deal, they are. When these are neglected over time, they can lead to health issues, psychological issues, and even more problems with self-esteem.

Though this might seem trite, sleep is incredibly important and vital for our physical and mental health. When we don't get enough sleep, we are more prone to illness, and we become less mentally prepared to handle stress, failure, and setbacks. Sleep really should be one of the prime focuses of any self-care routine.

We need to go to the doctor regularly to ensure that we are healthy and that no issues develop. This isn't necessarily easy as some people lack insurance or the financial means to obtain healthcare. If this applies to you, investigate community resources such as your local health department or any organizations dedicated to the health of its community members. This can put you in touch with low-cost or no-cost basic health services and may even provide access to low-cost mental health services.

We also must eat properly. The food we eat is the fuel our body uses to function and get us through our daily lives. Just like how putting bad fuel in a car makes it run less efficiently than it might otherwise, the same goes for us. We need to eat right, make sure we take time for important meals; that way, we aren't reaching for the chips while watching television in bed at night. As nice as it might seem, it isn't providing you with the fuel your body and mind need.

This can simply mean eating less sugar, making sure you are getting whole grains or cutting processed foods from your diet. These changes will have a significant positive impact on your health and improve your mental health and wellbeing.

Gut health is also important and something we don't give enough attention to. Helpful bacteria in the gut not only help aid in digestion, they aid in us getting the most nutrition out of our food, and there is evidence it can also contribute to our overall health. Getting healthy bacteria from your diet, such as by eating yogurt or drinking kombucha, is a great way to help keep your gut healthy.

We have all heard the adage about diet and exercise is the key component of health, and it is true. So now, we move on to exercise. You don't have to be a gym rat to get the benefits of exercise. Just a little activity like a short walk every day is more than enough. Keeping active helps keep you in shape and keep your internal organs operating optimally. And physical activity has been associated with reducing stress levels and aiding in sleep.

Now, we must move on to the less obvious parts of self-care. The first thing we need to address is our ability to say no. Most of us aren't flush with time, and the free time we have is valuable and should be used for things that enrich our lives. This is why we must learn how to say no and prioritize time for ourselves. It's helpful to block out personal time and be sure to stick to it.

Mostly, self-care should be enjoyable (exercise might be an exception here, but we still have to do it!) It helps to start with the basics and then move on to higher-order needs. When we have gotten enough sleep, practice good hygiene, and make time for ourselves, we are likely to find we feel better overall, and this makes us better equipped to handle the rigors of daily life.

We mentioned earlier that some people actually block out specific time for self-care and if it takes for that you to provide for your own needs and stick to it, you should do this. Self-care goes beyond things we need to do for ourselves and extends to things we should reserve the right to avoid and refuse. We must allow ourselves control over as many aspects of our life as we can, and while we can't avoid all frustrating interactions (nor should we), we do have a choice in which we face and which we don't.

Some people create a "no list" of things they won't participate in. It is okay to dig your heels in and refuse to participate in activities that aren't conducive to healthy self-esteem and positive interaction. There are some negative things we have no choice but to engage in, but you do not have to go to a dinner party that includes someone who always brings up negative topics and ruins the evening.

Being creative is a part of self-care that a lot of us neglect. You don't have to be a talented artist or musician to be creative. Listening to music, cooking, coloring, doing crafts, or even reading are all creative endeavors that engage your mind and provide you with a sense of enjoyment and wellbeing. These are not frivolous things; they are an integral part of a happy and healthy life. Humans are inherently creative beings, and a failure to address this part of our basic needs can make our lives less satisfying than they otherwise might be.

As we noted in the first chapter, distractions are not bad in and of themselves; try to find creative or fun distractions that give you a good way to pass the time or de-stress after a long day. Crafting or doing something mentally stimulating like a puzzle or a word game is a great way to unwind and still use your faculties. It isn't just mindless consumption.

The Internal Elements of Self-Care

As we have seen, self-care is a lot more than just making sure we get proper hydration. It also entails being more present and in the moment, which is what our creative endeavors and healthy distractions help to provide. We should also learn to pay closer attention to how we feel and about what we are thinking. This is part of the path to self-knowledge, self-awareness, and self-acceptance.

When we notice ourselves feeling something, especially something negative, we should take a pause and look at it deeper. Are our feelings warranted? Is it just the inner critic in our head with nothing better to do than make us feel bad about ourselves? Think about whether the sense of doubt or negative inner talk you are feeling is helpful to your current situation. If it is, pursue these thoughts. If it isn't, acknowledge that you felt that way and move on.

Psychologists recommend all these means of self-care to reduce stress, improve confidence, and raise overall feelings of general wellbeing. As we learn who we are and what we need, we can better plan personalized self-care routines that attend to our individual needs. We all are unique and require different things to live our best lives. Learning who we are and how to account for these varied needs is rewarding; it allows us to put our best self forward, which is better for the people around us.

Many people find it helpful to steal moments throughout the day for brief bouts of self-care. Taking a few minutes for positive affirmations or having a quick meditation session is a great way to keep our stress under control and make sure we are caring for ourselves. Self-care should mean allowing yourself the time and space to pursue the things you enjoy while also learning to love yourself.

Conclusion

Self-esteem is an important but complicated aspect of human life. Healthy self-esteem levels make it easier for someone to get what they want out of life and live a happy, healthy and fulfilled life, but this is far easier said than done since there are so many things that contribute to our feelings of personal value and worth. Plus, a high level of self-esteem is not necessarily a good thing in and of itself.

Like with mostly anything in life, balance and moderation are key. We want to have enough self-esteem that we value ourselves and can ask for the things we want and need, and take risks to make our lives better and more fulfilling. Conversely, we don't want so much self-esteem we come across as arrogant. That is an unattractive quality and not at all what we are looking to achieve.

We have a lot working against us when we are adults with low self-esteem. We often develop low self-esteem because of life experiences. Whether as a child or an adult, negative life experiences, and a lack of positive feedback can make us unsure of ourselves and doubt our value to the world. It is hard to get past life of bad experience, but with effort, self-reflection, self-compassion, and the ability to let go of the past, we can heal from these experiences and boost our self-esteem in the process.

Most of us barely know what self-esteem means and often misunderstand how to calculate the worth we place on ourselves. Our self-esteem refers to the value we give ourselves when compared to others, how worthy we feel we are of love and respect, the amount of confidence we have in our abilities, and more. Having low self-esteem can often mean we fear failure and risk so much we don't even bother trying; instead, we live a life dictated by fear and the whims of others. It is hard to be satisfied with this life.

There is a lot of work involved in developing healthy levels of self-esteem. First, we must learn about ourselves. We must understand whom we are, what we want, and what we need out of life. We must understand our emotions and take responsibility to form the impact our emotions and behavior have on our lives. Once we do this, we can see areas of our life where we can regain control and see the other elements we can improve so we can become the person we want to be.

Learning who we are can be a lifelong process. We are a mixture of thoughts and emotions, and many of us spend so much of our life on autopilot that we never really stop to ask ourselves why we feel the way we do or why we believe what we believe. But knowing this is important. It can help you learn how to best live a life based on your values and beliefs. It can also help you learn what you think, especially for those who have long had their opinions commanded by others. We might not always like what we see, but we must learn how to work on the aspects of ourselves we can control, how to forgive, and how to accept ourselves for the parts we cannot control. The path to healthy self-esteem requires a lot of forgiveness and letting go of the past. This applies to others, of course, but most importantly, *to us.*

We must do a lot more than take responsibility for our actions and figure out what we feel and why, we also must learn how to accept ourselves as we are. Yes, there are things we can control and change about ourselves, but there are other things we cannot change. Eventually, it is this that we must come to terms with if we want to love ourselves and let ourselves be loved. We must accept who and what we are and forgive ourselves for past mistakes, regrets, or roads not traveled.

Taking responsibility can be difficult and uncomfortable, but it is also empowering. It shows us there are many elements of our lives in which we can see a positive change because we have control over them. We must learn how to accept both the good and the bad, and that means we must take responsibility for the negative elements of our life we are responsible for. When we look closely at our lives, we will find areas of our lives and selves where we are abdicating responsibility onto someone else or some outside circumstance.

We must learn about distraction and why we choose it at certain times. Then, we must learn how to regain control over it so we are living life in the present and are actually "there" rather than on autopilot. A lot of what is entailed in improving our self-esteem is difficult, uncomfortable, and it takes time, but the effort is definitely worth it. Distraction keeps us from being present in our daily lives and can have a negative impact on our relationships when we aren't fully engaged with the world. Most of us do this without even knowing we are doing it; we do it mindlessly.

Distraction, like so much of what we talked about in this book, is not something to be avoided, but, we need to be more conscious of and in control. There is nothing inherently wrong with distraction, and it serves a really good purpose in allowing us moments of freedom from the rigors of life. That said, there must be a balance. We must allow ourselves distractions, but consciously so. We must know that we are using distractions and that we have a good reason for doing it.

A big part of gaining self-esteem is learning how to live in the present and becoming cognizant of what is going on around you. This will make it easier for you to read a situation and pick up nonverbal cues you might otherwise miss. Plus, it will mean you are actually present in your social interactions. It's hard to listen to your spouse tell a story about their day when you are also scrolling through social media at the same. It not only makes it hard to pay attention, but it also sends a clear message to your partner they are not getting your full attention, and that isn't something we should want them to feel.

A vital component of all of this is developing a positive level of assertiveness. This, of course, does not mean becoming overbearing and dominating, but, developing the ability to ask for what you need and make sure your opinion is heard. It involves you taking ownership of your feelings and learning to express them in positive ways. It isn't easy to develop self-assertiveness because many of us have a lifetime of letting others direct the ins and outs of our lives. Some of us also come from cultures where certain groups of people (like women) are not raised to be assertive, and it may even lead to negative consequences in their lives.

We also must step back and look at our social circle and think about who we are friends with and why. We need to make sure our support networks comprise people who you love and respect and who love and respect you. Sometimes becoming more confident will require you to reduce the influence certain people have over your life if they aren't affecting it in a positive way. As the name implies, a support network should offer you positive support in your time of need, as you should provide them the same in return. Relationships of all types should be mutually beneficial and not a competition.

It is also important to think about whom we compare ourselves to and why. This is why we have to look closely at our social media use and focus on celebrity culture. These things can be fun and harmless in small doses, but research shows that too much focus on these things has a negative effect on our feelings of value and worth. Remember, it is imperative we manage this so it either has a positive impact or no impact on our life.

When we realize that we are using social media in an unhealthy way (detrimental to our feelings of self-worth and value), we either need to adjust how we view and see social media or remove ourselves from it entirely. Few people will live a life without social media because it is a great way to keep up with friends and family and engage with others who share our interests. This is fine, but we must look closely at our usage to ensure this is actually what we are doing with our time on social media.

Though it might not seem like a huge deal, social media can have a profound impact on our lives and how we feel we stack up against other people. Thus, it is vitally important to find a healthy way to use social media, or you may have to withdraw from it for periods of time. Some people take "screen breaks" where they don't look at social media for a weekend here and there. This can be a great way to get your head out of that unrealistic virtual space and get yourself re-centered in the real world with more realistic expectations.

So much of developing our self-esteem requires us to learn and figure out how to control what we can accept and what we can't. It also requires us to develop confidence in our thoughts, feelings, and ideas so we can express them and act when necessary. One way we can help our confidence, and our lives, is to participate in something bigger than ourselves.

When we involve ourselves with a hobby, cause, or organization that goes beyond our own little existence, we find meaning and purpose in life that many think of as one of the defining features of human life. Not only will this help you live your life by your values, but it also takes away reasons for your inner critic to rear its ugly head and fill you with negative self-thought. It is also rewarding and a positive thing for the world.

Learning how to care for ourselves physically, mentally, and spiritually is something that we must work on for a lifetime. Finding ways to be more present and live a more mindful life helps us reduce stress, improve our sense of physical and mental wellbeing, and foster good health. Taking care of ourselves, whether by meditating regularly or making sure we get enough sleep, will go a long way towards helping us become better able to handle stress and negativity, which often work to better our self-esteem.

Taking care of oneself is not selfish. It is hard to love others openly and provide something of value to the world when we aren't even willing to properly defer our own basic life needs. Loving ourselves makes us better friends, partners, coworkers, and more.

All these things will take time, but the result will be worth it since the result is the ability to gain self-love and self-respect. Self-esteem is a varied and complex subject with a lot of variables that factor into how we feel about ourselves. If we want to improve our self-esteem, it will take a lot of work and conscious effort, but it is possible to allow ourselves love and forgiveness and to strive towards becoming that person we know we are inside.

Here's another book by Mark Jeffers that you might like

Unlock the Secrets to a Stoic Life, Emotional Resilience and an Unshakeable Mindset

Discover Principles, Mindful Meditation Techniques and Habits for Bulletproof Calmness in Chaos

References

A Nice Person's Guide to Becoming Assertive. (2020). Mindforlife.Org. https://www.mindforlife.org/nice-persons-guide-becoming-assertive/

Ackerman, C. (2018, November 6). What is Self-Worth and How Do We Increase it? (Incl. 4 Worksheets). PositivePsychology.Com. https://positivepsychology.com/self-worth/

Ackerman, C. (2019, July 3). What is Self-Awareness and Why is it Important? [+5 Ways to Increase It]. PositivePsychology.Com. https://positivepsychology.com/self-awareness-matters-how-you-can-be-more-self-aware/

Assertiveness | Psychology Today. (2019). Psychology Today.

https://www.psychologytoday.com/us/basics/assertiveness

Baratta, M. (2018). Self Care 101. Psychology Today. https://www.psychologytoday.com/us/blog/skinny-revisited/201805/self-care-101

Baumeister, R. F., Campbell, J. D., Krueger, J. I., & Vohs, K. D. (2003). Does High Self-Esteem Cause Better Performance, Interpersonal Success, Happiness, or Healthier Lifestyles? Psychological Science in the Public Interest, 4(1), 1–44. https://journals.sagepub.com/doi/10.1111/1529-1006.01431

Beach, J. (2017, June 6). Why People Who Have a Life Purpose Have Higher Self-Esteem. Lifehack. https://www.lifehack.org/597693/why-people-who-have-a-life-purpose-have-higher-self-esteem

Boyes, A. (2018, June 19). 5 Self-Sabotaging Things Unconfident People Do. Psychology Today. https://www.psychologytoday.com/us/blog/in-practice/201806/5-self-sabotaging-things-unconfident-people-do

Brockway, J. (2019, December 9). The 31 Absolute Best Body Positivity Moments of 2019. Good Housekeeping; Good Housekeeping. https://www.goodhousekeeping.com/health/wellness/g28497513/body-positivity-moments-2019/

Brown, M. (2019, May 18). 9 Signs of Low Self-Esteem & 10 Ways Grow Confidence. The Couch: A Therapy & Mental Wellness Blog. https://blog.zencare.co/boost-self-esteem/

Bruening, L. (2019, October 19). Personal Responsibility and Mental Health. Psychology Today. https://www.psychologytoday.com/us/blog/your-neurochemical-self/201910/personal-responsibility-and-mental-health

Burgess, J. (2019, November 25). 21 powerful positive affirmations for confidence and self-esteem. Life Sorted. https://www.lifesorted.com/positive-affirmations-for-confidence/

Burton, N. (2012). Building Confidence and Self-Esteem. Psychology Today. https://www.psychologytoday.com/us/blog/hide-and-seek/201205/building-confidence-and-self-esteem

Caiola, R. (2016, October 25). 8 Ways To Practice Self-Acceptance. HuffPost. https://www.huffpost.com/entry/8-ways-to-practice-self-acceptance_b_12640812

Davis, T. (2018). Self-Care: 12 Ways to Take Better Care of Yourself. Psychology Today. https://www.psychologytoday.com/us/blog/click-here-happiness/201812/self-care-12-ways-take-better-care-yourself

Deep H, O. P. for. (2018, February 6). 7 skills of self-responsibility. Medium. https://medium.com/what-is-the-real-cause-of-depression/7-skills-of-self-responsibility-bb882edd506b

DW, J. (2018, April 13). 30 Affirmations for Confidence. Jessica DW | Spiritual Leadership Coach. https://jessicadw.com/blog/2018/4/13/30-affirmations-for-confidence

Eurich, T. (2018, April 23). What Self-Awareness Really Is (and How to Cultivate It). Harvard Business Review. https://hbr.org/2018/01/what-self-awareness-really-is-and-how-to-cultivate-it

Free Relaxation Script: Self-Esteem Relaxation. (n.d.). Www.Innerhealthstudio.Com. https://www.innerhealthstudio.com/self-esteem-relaxation.html

Friedman, W. J. (2015). Self-Responsibility/Self-Accountability Qualifies You as an Adult - Wellness, Disease Prevention, And Stress Reduction Information. Mentalhelp.Net. https://www.mentalhelp.net/blogs/self-responsibility-self-accountability-qualifies-you-as-an-adult/

Friendman, W. J. (2016, January 21). The importance of self-responsibility. Red Deer Advocate. https://www.reddeeradvocate.com/life/the-importance-of-self-responsibility/

Fuller, J. R. (2015, March 27). Social Media Use and Self-Esteem. New York Behavioral Health. https://newyorkbehavioralhealth.com/social-media-use-and-self-esteem/

Graf, S. (2020, September 17). How to Meditate for Self Discovery. WikiHow. https://www.wikihow.com/Meditate-for-Self-Discovery

Hill, J. (2019, December 11). What Is Self-Worth and How to Recognize Yours. Lifehack. https://www.lifehack.org/854916/what-is-self-worth

How to Be Assertive Asking for What You Want Firmly and Fairly. (2009). Mindtools.Com. https://www.mindtools.com/pages/article/Assertiveness.htm

How to Build Confidence Through Meditation | How to Beast. (n.d.). How to Beast. Retrieved from https://www.howtobeast.com/build-confidence-meditation/

How to Build Your Self-Worth When No One Taught You How. (n.d.). Tiffany Writes Things. Retrieved from https://www.tiffanywritesthings.com/personal-development/2018/11/1/how-to-build-your-self-worth-when-no-one-taught-you-how

https://www.facebook.com/FrankSonnenbergOnline. (2014, December 16). 7 Ways To Live Life With a Purpose. Frank Sonnenberg Online. https://www.franksonnenbergonline.com/blog/7-ways-to-live-life-with-a-purpose/

https://www.facebook.com/verywell. (2019). 5 Ways to Start Boosting Your Self-Confidence Today. Verywell Mind.

https://www.verywellmind.com/how-to-boost-your-self-confidence-4163098

Improving Assertiveness Self-Help Resources - Information Sheets. (n.d.). Www.Cci.Health.Wa.Gov.Au. https://www.cci.health.wa.gov.au/Resources/Looking-After-Yourself/Assertiveness

Maier, R. (2018). Self-Responsibility: Transformations. American Behavioral Scientist, 63(1), 27–42. https://journals.sagepub.com/doi/10.1177/0002764218816802

Manson, M. (2018, May 3). The Three Levels of... Mark Manson; Mark Manson. https://markmanson.net/self-awareness

Marie, K., & Williams, B. (2020). Self-awareness theory and decision theory: a theoretical and empirical integration. https://core.ac.uk/download/pdf/38917907.pdf

Mayo Clinic Staff. (2017). Stressed out? Be assertive. Mayo Clinic. https://www.mayoclinic.org/healthy-lifestyle/stress-management/in-depth/assertive/art-20044644

McCarthy, M. (n.d.). Why strong self-esteem is the secret to success in life. Www.Createwritenow.Com. https://www.createwritenow.com/journal-writing-blog/why-strong-self-esteem-is-the-secret-to-success-in-life

Meditation: In Depth. (n.d.). NCCIH. https://www.nccih.nih.gov/health/meditation-in-depth

Michael, R. (2018, July 8). What Self-Care Is — and What It Isn't. World of Psychology. https://psychcentral.com/blog/what-self-care-is-and-what-it-isnt-2/

Miller, K. D. (2020, January 7). Using Self-Awareness Theory and Skills in Psychology. PositivePsychology.Com. https://positivepsychology.com/self-awareness-theory-skills/

Moore, C. (2019, March 4). Positive Daily Affirmations: Is There Science Behind It? PositivePsychology.Com. https://positivepsychology.com/daily-affirmations/

Morin, A. (2017, July 11). How Do You Measure Your Self-Worth? Psychology Today. https://www.psychologytoday.com/us/blog/what-mentally-strong-people-dont-do/201707/how-do-you-measure-your-self-worth

Olatunbosun, M. (2018, November 7). 13 Ways Living with Purpose Makes You Happier and More Fulfilled. Lifehack. https://www.lifehack.org/814085/living-with-purpose

Pillay, S. (2016, May 16). Greater self-acceptance improves emotional well-being - Harvard Health Blog. Harvard Health Blog. https://www.health.harvard.edu/blog/greater-self-acceptance-improves-emotional-well-201605169546

Powell, A. (2018, April 9). Harvard researchers study how mindfulness may change the brain in depressed patients. Harvard Gazette; Harvard Gazette. https://news.harvard.edu/gazette/story/2018/04/harvard-researchers-study-how-mindfulness-may-change-the-brain-in-depressed-patients/

Raghunathan, R. (2011, December 14). Take Personal Responsibility, Don't Blame Others. Psychology Today. https://www.psychologytoday.com/us/blog/sapient-nature/201112/take-personal-responsibility-dont-blame-others

Ravenscraft, E. (2019, June 3). Practical Ways to Improve Your Confidence (and Why You Should). The New York Times. https://www.nytimes.com/2019/06/03/smarter-living/how-to-improve-self-confidence.html

Robins, R. W., & Trzesniewski, K. H. (2005). Self-Esteem Development Across the Lifespan. Current Directions in Psychological Science, 14(3), 158–162. https://journals.sagepub.com/doi/10.1111/j.0963-7214.2005.00353.x

Schwitzgebel, E. (2010). Introspection (Stanford Encyclopedia of Philosophy). Stanford.Edu. https://plato.stanford.edu/entries/introspection/

Self-Care. (n.d.). Active Minds. https://www.activeminds.org/about-mental-health/self-care/

Self-Esteem | Psychology Today. (2019). Psychology Today. https://www.psychologytoday.com/us/basics/self-esteem

Setlzer, L. (2011). The Path to Unconditional Self-Acceptance. Psychology Today. https://www.psychologytoday.com/us/blog/evolution-the-self/200809/the-path-unconditional-self-acceptance

Smith, J., Suttie, J., Jazaieri, H., & Newman, K. (2018, November 12). 10 Things We Know About the Science of Meditation - Mindful.

Mindful. https://www.mindful.org/10-things-we-know-about-the-science-of-meditation/

Sokal, J. (2011, August 30). What You Need to Live a Life of Purpose. Tiny Buddha. https://tinybuddha.com/blog/what-you-need-to-live-a-life-of-purpose/

Tartakovsky, M., & read, M. S. L. updated: 8 O. 2018~ 4 min. (2016, May 17). Therapists Spill: 12 Ways to Accept Yourself. Psychcentral.Com. https://psychcentral.com/lib/therapists-spill-12-ways-to-accept-yourself/

Taylor, J. (2010, June 7). Popular Culture: America's Self-esteem Problem. Psychology Today. https://www.psychologytoday.com/us/blog/the-power-prime/201006/popular-culture-americas-self-esteem-problem

The Importance of Self-Worth - PsychAlive. (2014, May 9). PsychAlive. https://www.psychalive.org/self-worth/

Tucker-Ladd, C. (2010, February 25). Building Assertiveness in 4 Steps. World of Psychology. https://psychcentral.com/blog/building-assertiveness-in-4-steps/

Why Self-Esteem is Important and Its Dimensions. (2015). Mentalhelp.Net. https://www.mentalhelp.net/self-esteem/why-its-important/

Wignall, N. (2019, March 15). Assertiveness: A Step-by-Step Guide to Becoming More Assertive [2020]. Nick Wignall. https://nickwignall.com/assertiveness/

Laurie Santos' Yale "Happiness" course (The Science of Well-Being) is available for free on Coursera (https://www.coursera.org/learn/the-science-of-well-being#). It's well worth listening to the lectures and picking a few of the recommended books, if you want to do further reading.

Monash University, in Australia, has a great psychology department which has created several MOOCs on mindfulness and well-being as well as other topics like the psychology of learning. Their courses can be found at

https://www.futurelearn.com/partners/monash-university, and most are free to follow.

Jen Sincero's *You are a Badass* is a book which takes a refreshingly down to Earth and sometimes quite profane attitude to positive thinking. If you're fed up with motivational posters showing pretty sunsets and cute kittens, this might be a good book for you. There's also a follow-up book analyzing the problems many people have with their relationship to money and adopting a positive thinking approach to solving those problems.

Buddhist monastic Venerable Amy Miller (amymiller.com) has an excellent YouTube channel giving in-depth analysis of certain meditative practices. While she belongs specifically to the Tibetan Mahayana tradition, the principles she talks about in the videos are applicable to those of any spirituality or indeed none.

A number of apps exist for tablets and smartphones which can help you keep a regular positive thinking or meditation practice. Many of them are either free or freemium. Smiling Mind, Headspace, and Insight Timer are among the best of these apps.